GUARANTEED ADMISSION INTO GOD'S

YOUR PASSPORT TO HEAVEN

DIANE TESSMAN & TIMOTHY GREEN BECKLEY

YOUR PASSPORT TO HEAVEN
by Diane Tessman
and
Timothy Green Beckley

ISBN: 0-938294-88-1

Editorial Direction:

Timothy Green Beckley

& Carol Ann Rodriguez

Composition and design:
Cross-Country Consultants
8858 E. Palm Ridge Drive
Scottsdale, AZ 85260

For permission to reprint specific portions or to inquire
about foreign rights, address request to Inner Light, Box 753,
New Brunswick, NJ 08903

Free catalog of books upon request.

CONTENTS

**Diane Tessman and Timothy Green Beckley,
authors, *Your Passport to Heaven***

Diane Tessman is the head of the Starlite Mystic Center in St. Ansgar, Iowa, from which she publishes a variety of newsletters and publications. She is the author of *Earth Changes Bible* and *Seven Rays of the Healing Millennium*. A noted channel and New Age philosopher, her work has been accredited by such authorities as Ruth Montgomery. She can be reached at Box 352, St. Ansgar, IA 50472. Readers may write for a publication list.

Timothy Green Beckley is a veteran investigator of UFOs and other unexplained phenomena. In addition to being the editor of the nationally distributed magazines *UFO Universe* and *Unsolved UFO Sightings,* he is the president of Inner Light Publications and author of such works as *MJ-12 and the Riddle of Hangar 18, Subterranean Worlds Inside Earth, Psychic and UFO Revelations in the Last Days* and various other works. He can be reached in care of Inner Light Publications, Box 753, New Brunswick, NJ 08903. A free catalog is available upon request.

The Heaven's Gate Tragedy: A Tragic Tie-in and Possible Meaning

■ What do Heaven and UFOs really have to do with each other?

■ Who—if anybody—should be blamed for the tragic situation in which 39 people took their own lives because they believed that they were simply their earthly bodies ("containers," they called them), to return to their starship which they believed was traveling behind the Hale-Bopp Comet?

Before giving our answers to these important questions, it should be noted that the mass media jumped on this unfortunate event like hungry barracudas, digging into the fact that some male members of the Heaven's Gate group were surgically castrated. Immediately, the press put a negative slant on anything to do with this "cult," including the fact that its leader had once been involved in a gay relationship when he was a college music professor, and that he had met his "soulmate" in a mental institution.

Regardless of how one personally feels about gay relationships, it is certain that the media hits new heights in hypocrisy when, in one breath, they give "politically correct" lip service to the right of consenting adults to love whom they please, and with the next breath, smirk about the fact the group's leader, named Do (formerly known as Bo) had a homosexual relationship years previously and felt guilty about it. And while men of all faiths and denominations have had to tangle with such "demons," isn't it, in reality, the so-called orthodox religions—and not the supposed cult

6

groups—that makes us feel guilty and insecure when it comes to our own individual sexuality? So much so, that it is not that uncommon for the religiously inclined to take matters into their own hands and torture themselves either spiritually or physically due to their own individual leanings. The same media—as well as those who consider themselves to be "cult hunters"—neglect to mention it is they who originally drove the group's leader into a mental institution because they didn't understand his fascination with UFOs and extraterrestrials. Sometimes, society can "condemn" us without reasonable cause, simply because they do not possess the knowledge to deal with what they see as differences of opinion and individual thinking that may go against what is at that time considered to be the "norm."

Can we also—in all honesty—hold our own government to blame? It would seem that they may be in reality a cause of the hysteria that has grown up around the whole idea of UFOs, simply because for the last half a century they have decided it is their duty to hide the truth from the public for its "own protection." Because of this factor, society has had to formulate its own preconceptions and conclusions about something which they inwardly know to be real (due to personal observation and experience). Many of us have a tough time dealing with something which society's great institutions tell us we should shun...the same institutions we have been lead to believe are always infallible.

On the video's which were left behind, Do's followers—known as "monks" —appear to be very intelligent and enlightened, to have a great sense of humor and camaraderie. Yet, we are told that they are kooks and crackpots. The fundamental question must be: Why does society condemn such people outright, even making them the brunt of sad jokes, while at the same time traditional Christian beliefs are based around a man who was ostracized in his time, a man who had fiercely devoted followers, a man who was more intelligent, enlightened, and gentle than the world around him?

Traditional Christianity teaches us that if you are good, you will go to heaven, which is a place of perfection where none of the worldly woes exist. Heaven is "up there" somewhere, amongst the stars, comets and planets. Catholic monks and nuns are considered by some to be very worthy spiritual people. But apparently, there is a "copyright" on who can be a monk. If you are not of a huge, multi- billionaire dollar church conglomerate, your right to consider yourself a "monk" is not valid because then you are just a cult member. This is what we are repeatedly being told, but is this necessarily true? What separates the big churches from the cults—is it the number of followers and the amount of their bank balance which determines our feelings toward them? A century or so ago the Mormons were considered to be a cult (remember how their leader Joseph Smith was persecuted?), while today they are thought of in much more "traditional" terms.

Heaven Abounds for the Faithful

When someone passes on, traditional belief tells us to rejoice, that he or she has gone on to a higher place. But when Heaven's Gate members die, video cameras cruelly, obstructively scan their lifeless physical forms, and narrators sorrowfully tell us how pitiful their deaths are. We are told that they are dead as dead can be, that their plans to go to a higher place were nothing but a big deception.

What if someone were to say such negative things about a person at a traditional funeral? Every aspect of Heavens Gate's beliefs have been ridiculed and dissected. Isn't it time society learned to be more tolerant of a person's independence that might take them away from the norm? After all, isn't individuality what America is supposed to be all about?

Perhaps this double standard is the very thing Heavens Gate members found wrong with society. Perhaps this is why they chose to live together in a monastery away from the world that had rejected them and their beliefs out of hand.

We do not feel that society should condone or condemn others without having spent a day in their shoes. Traditionally, we have been taught that suicide is wrong, but should we not be sympathetic with the hurt and anger which anyone who considers suicide must feel?

It seems, like Heaven's Gate members should have stayed on Earth to assist in this planet's transformation period, which is likely to be the greatest crisis civilization has ever gone through. It would seem that they "deserted" right when we needed their enlightenment, intelligence and gentleness, the most.

Despite all our thoughts, we must still ask the question: Can a UFO take us to heaven? This little book attempts to answer this and other relevant questions that are all too important as we enter these final days before the change of the millennium.

Many do not comprehend that there are indeed various levels of consciousness. Quantum physics tells us about multi-dimensions and there is now even "scientific" proof that different, various realms abound throughout the cosmos.

Every individual must learn to cherish his or her freedom of choice.

To truly accomplish a higher consciousness, free will must be present. There can be no cult leader who says he or she is your savior. You must learn that your savior is within yourself! Look to spiritual teachers and friends, if you must, for guidance and input, but do not let them dictate to you. Do NOT let them demand to be worshiped.

You are your own country and as such, you have the right to issue your own Passport to Heaven!

Such actions as mass suicide, in our view, do not lend themselves to evolving to a higher consciousness. To place your sacred life force in a leader's hands is not an act of wisdom or higher awareness, but a cop-out.

In this book, the authors give you insight on what are undoubtedly the most fascinating, urgent questions of today:

■ Is there life after death? ■ Are there other realms of existence ■ And how can a person get to the higher most places?

In this time of planetary crisis, these questions haunt us more and more. Millions of people have seen and encountered UFOs, so we are not in a position to laugh at them any more.

■ Do these craft return to the higher levels of existence once they leave Earth? ■ Have the occupants of UFOs—whom some identify as aliens, and others recognize as angels—graduated to a realm which is more heavenly beyond our daily existence? ■ And is it possible we can join them?

The deaths in San Diego make us ask these questions with even more curiosity and a sense of urgency.

What must each and every one of us know, feel and believe, as the millennium draws to a crashing close? Allow us to tell you about Your Passport to Heaven!

Diane Tessmann
P.O.Box 352
St. Ansgar, IA 50472

We ask you read this book with an open mind and appreciate all comments meant in good faith, while rejecting all that come in negativity. The angelic kingdom awaits us all and our personal guardian angels are here to offer protection and guidance.

No one can benefit from close minded ignorance.

Timothy Green Beckley
P.O Box 753
New Brunswick, NJ 08903

Life—Not Death—After Life!

There is no doubt the heavens await...

Bright angels have from glory come;
They're round my bed, they're in my room,
They wait to waft my spirit home!
    All is well! All is well!

In the course of the author's spiritual counseling work, we have had many letters from people wondering if there is indeed life after death. Very often these people have just lost a loved one and they seek hope and encouragement on the phenomenon of "death" and the afterlife.

We have both also been in touch with other people telling of their own life after death experiences. In some cases, they tell of their own near death, of the glorious other world they saw, and of their reluctant return to life in this dimension. In other instances, they tell of their personal experiences following the death of a loved one, of how the loved one reappeared from the other dimension in order to let the person left behind know that there is indeed life—not death—after life!

Science and Religion in Harmony

It is the hope of Tim Beckley and Diane Tessman that this book will give the reader reassurance that the spirit does not cease to exist. Both science and religion now appear to agree on this point. Consider the fact that Albert Einstein revealed that *energy* cannot be destroyed, it can only be changed into other forms. Also consider the fact that *all* spiritual beliefs in the world, be they eastern or western, Christian or non-Christian, teach us that *life* is a sacred and undestroyable energy. All religions tell us, in various terms, that the special essence unique to each individual called "the soul" does live on. Some beliefs tell us that the soul goes to the dimension of heaven, while other beliefs tell us that the soul is reborn into another physical being, to continue its journey through the cosmos. The details of where the soul goes and what it does after death do vary, but the basic fact that the soul does not die is *universal*. And so, science and religion both reassure us, despite their different terminology, that there is life after death—but can we have a real and true picture of exactly what does happen? Let's see what science and religion have to say.

A Scientist Offers Proof of Survival

At some time in their life everyone is asked the question: Do you believe you will go on living after you die?

Well, do you believe it?

Consider the facts. Time after time people have reported that a dying person's face is suddenly filled with HAPPINESS at the actual moment of death.

Is it possible to know WHY?

Yes. Through the people who have experienced "death"—and come back to tell the story.

This enquiry begins with the documented evidence of a scientist.

He has made the most careful study yet of WHAT HAPPENS WHEN PEOPLE DIE.

He is Dr. Robert Crookall, who lives in Dursley, Gloucestershire.

He has probed and sifted through all the cases he could track down. Here are some of them:

CASE of the man who lost a bond acknowledging a debt of money. Without the bond he could not legally demand repayment. His debtor repudiated the claim.

Then he was almost drowned. Scene by scene his life passed before him—INCLUDING THE MOMENT WHEN HE HAD HIDDEN THE BOND IN A SECRET PLACE.

When he recovered he went to his bookcase, took out a book...and extracted the bond.

CASE of Flight-Lieut. J.P. Wynton. He described to Dr. Crookall how HE experienced a timeless review of his life as he crashed in a plane and was almost burnt to death.

But from the pilot and others Dr. Cookall made a new and strange discovery.

Time after time people snatched from violent death told him that as death approached they felt no pain.

His theory was confirmed, for example, by one:

CASE of Leslie Grant Scott.

"Dying is not such a terrifying thing," said Mr. Scott.

"I died and came back. I found death one of the easiest things in life."

Or, again, consider:

CASE of a man who fell from a tremendous height. He said:

"When my body finally bounded against the rocks...I became unconscious without experiencing any pain whatever. The moments when I stood at the brink of the (new) life were the happiest I ever experienced."

Dr. Crookall also listened to the:

CASE of a doctor who fell a hundred feet, heard the noise when his head struck various corners of rocks, but stated:

"In all this I felt no pain."

This only came later when he re-entered his body.

These cases, and many others were published in a book, written by Dr. Crookall, called *The Supreme Adventure.*

Dr. Crookall is a scientist. He has been demonstrator in botany at Aberdeen University and Principal Geologist to Her Majesty's Geological Survey. He likes to go about things in a scientific way.

He decided that we were looking for proof of survival in the wrong place. That if we wanted evidence about the next world we should look for it there, not in verifiable memories of this world.

He began by collecting communications from the "dead" by whatever means they came.

He examined thousands of accounts of what these allegedly dead people said they experienced at, and soon after, death.

From these he was able to build up the first consistent and coherent account of how those who have been through death say they pass from this world to the next.

This is the amazing picture which emerged:

1. In addition to his Physical Body, man also has a Psychical or Soul Body which we cannot see or touch but which has the same shape as the physical body. And there is another Spiritual Body, too, on a higher level still.

2. As a man approaches a natural death, at old age, his thoughts fly instinctively to friends who have died already. He summons them to help him over to the next stage.

3. Near the moment of death man experiences a detailed review of

his past earthly life.

4. About an hour before visible death, when the heart stops beating and he ceases to breathe, a dying man has often already left his physical body and stands nearby conscious and happy.

This is what we call the pre-death coma.

5. Natural death involves no physical pain or fear.

6. Many of the newly dead do not, for a time, realize that they have shed their physical bodies.

7. The psychical double that leaves the physical body at death usually floats for a while horizontally above the dead physical body, resembles it, and looks younger and brighter,.

8. Many of the newly dead see immediately friends who have died already, especially those whom they have unconsciously called.

9. When he has severed the final links with his physical body, the average man who dies naturally has a recuperative sleep lasting for three or four days of our time.

But a man who is killed in the prime of life tends to be awake at once.

10. The next world in which he finds himself is not, as is taught in some churches, of a purely spiritual nature, or the Paradise of the Bible. That comes later.

The next world for the average man is semi-physical in nature: intermediate between our earth and the "Heaven" of the Scriptures. It is earth-like and familiar.

11. During the period which follows, the newly dead man experiences a second review of his past earth life. This time emotional, selective and responsible. It is the Biblical "Judgement."

12. On the basis of this each person goes eventually to his own place in the spiritual or super-physical heavens. These cannot be described in normal language, but they are more real than the physical world.

Sudden or Violent Death

But what happens to the people who die a sudden or violent death?

They suffer from shock, says Dr. Crookall. For them it is difficult to realize what happened.

But with help, after a period of rest in special conditions after death, they are ready to join the normal sequence.

The first question Dr. Crookall asked—as a scientist—was:

"DOES IT MAKE SENSE?"

He found that it does.

More than that, he found the communications he tested were consistent with one another.

Then he discovered something even more conclusive.

It was possible to test the sensations said to be experienced by newly dead people by comparing them with sensations known to have been experienced by people who have returned from near death to physical life.

The communications from the dead said that they actually left their bodies about an hour before the heart stopped beating.

And that while they were still linked by the invisible cord to their physical bodies, it was always possible to return to them.

During this period people who did return, and are alive today, have experienced some of the first stages of the transition from this life to the next.

That's where these cases we showed you at the start come in.

For these experiences are similar, usually identical to those described by the dead.

Many people who have "died" and come back have described how they left their physical body and looked down on it.

And this has been corroborated by people who have never been near death themselves but have seen it happen while watching others die. Let us examine another case:

CASE of an American doctor, R.B. Hout, of Indiana. At the deathbed of his aunt he saw "this astral body hang suspended horizontally a few feet above the physical counterpart:

"It was quiet, serene and in repose. But the physical body was active in reflex movements and subconscious writhings of pain.

"I saw the features plainly. They were very similar to the physical face except that a glow of peace and vigour was expressed instead of age and pain.

"My uncle, the deceased husband of my aunt, stood there beside her bed. Also her son, passed away many years previously."

This phase—the arrival of friends or relatives already dead—has been corroborated by almost everyone who has seen death often.

Time after time the dying person's face is suddenly filled with happiness at the actual moment of death.

Sometimes they even speak the name of a friend or relation who has died before.

Crookall found that "there seems to be no single case on record in which a dying person claimed to see a living friend whom he erroneously thought to be dead.

"On the other hand there are many recorded cases of dying people who saw friends whom they supposed to be living and who were in fact dead."

Doctors are so used to this phenomenon that some have come to expect death soon after their patients appear to see friends who have died.

A Nurse's Experience

And a nurse with twenty years experience has testified:

"I notice that often just before the end, the dying would seem to recognize someone who was not of those at the bedside and who was unseen by the latter.

"I have seen a woman who had been in a coma for hours suddenly open her eyes with a look of glad surprise, stretch forth her hands as though to grasp invisible hands outstretched towards her, and then, with a sigh of relief, expire.

"That at such moments the dying really see some spirit form—someone who has come from the other world to welcome them—I have never doubted."

Perhaps you are one of those who are in doubt.

Everyone who believes in Christianity should, as an act of faith, believe that they will survive their own death.

Yet, recent surveys have revealed that more than half the people of Britain have no conviction at all.

Faith, and the evidence of the Bible are no longer enough. They want proof.

Others like the nurse and Dr. Hout, of Indiana, who have come face to face with the evidence have no more doubts.

And Dr. Crookall, in the face of the body of evidence he has amassed, was unable to doubt either.

"The whole of the available evidence," he concludes, "is explicable only on the hypothesis of the survival of the human soul in a Soul Body.

"There is no longer a deadlock or stalemate on the question of survival.

"On the contrary, survival is as well established as the theory of evolution."

Other Scientists Report their Observations

The majority of the readers of this book are probably very familiar with the fine research work done by Raymond A. Moody, Jr., M.D. whose book *Life After Life* topped the best seller list several years ago. Yet, these same readers may not be familiar with the excellent investigative techniques applied by other men of science, who though they might have started out as skeptics, are now convinced of survival.

Take as an example the investigation conducted by Dr. Kenneth Ring, a professor of psychology at the University of Connecticut. As co-founder and First Vice-President of the Association for the Scientific Study of Near-Death Phenomena, Dr. Ring has interviewed more than a hundred men and women who have come very close to death or have experienced what is termed "clinical death," that is a state in which vital signs such as heartbeat and respiration have been entirely absent from their bodies.

In his book *Life at Death* (Coward, McCann & Geoghegan), Dr. Ring confirms the findings made by researchers before him in this area, including the following sensations which have commonly been associated with those undergoing a near death experience:

■ A sense of floating out of one's body.

■ The feeling of flying through a dark tunnel at whose end there is a brilliant white light.

■ Experiencing a review of one's life, the scenes flashing before the mind's eye in rapid order.

Not quick to draw conclusions of his own, Dr. Ring does seem adequately impressed by the weight of experience he has seen and in his first literary effort he shows that the near-death experience is not affected by an individual's age, education, race or religion. He found instead that the typical near-death experience—which he terms a "core experience"—tends to unfold in a series of five stages. The "deeper" the stage, the fewer the people who reach it. The experience tends, Dr. Ring maintains, to end with an encounter with what is often described as a "voice" or "presence" that asks whether the person wants to return to life. The after effects of this "core experience" are dramatic and profound. As described in *Life at Death* the fear of death tends to vanish, and the total impact is akin to a spiritual rebirth.

The conclusions Dr. Ring has reached are very dramatic when one considers that they are coming from a man of science who does not dare reach conclusions until he has tallied up all the evidence. "I do believe— but not just on the basis of my own or other's data regarding near-death experience—that we continue to have a conscious existence after our physical death and that the core experience does represent its beginning, a sort of glimpse of things to come. I am, in fact, convinced—both from my own personal experiences and from my studies as a psychologist—that it is possible to become conscious of 'other realities' and that the coming close to death represents one avenue to a higher 'frequency domain,' or reality, which will be fully accessible to us following what we call death." As far as Dr. Ring is concerned, the near-death experience is important not only to the person that has undergone it, but he sees a far more important implication in such experiences which he feels are meant to have a profound impact on society as a whole.

"My own understanding of these near-death experiences leads me to regard them as 'teachings.' They are, it seems to me, by their nature, revelatory experiences. They vouchsafe both to those who undergo them and to those who hear about them an intuitive sense of the transcendent aspect of creation. These experiences clearly imply that there is something more, something beyond the physical world of the senses, which, in the light of these experiences, now appears to be only the mundane segment of a greater spectrum of reality."

And why are such experiences seemingly increasing in number at this time in our history? Dr. Ring has a speculative answer which can be justified in light of some other theories that will be discussed later on in this book. "I have come to believe," states the astute author, "that the universe has many ways of 'getting its message across.' In a sense, it wants us to 'wake up,' to become aware of the cosmic dimensions of the drama of which we are all a part. Near-death experiences represent one of its devices for waking us up to this higher reality. The 'message'—for the experiencing individual at least—is usually so clear, potent, and undeniable that it is neither forgotten nor dismissed. Potentially, then, those who have these experiences become 'prophets' to the rest of us who have fallen back to sleep or have never been awaken. From this point of view, the voices we have heard are those of prophets preaching a religion of universal brotherhood and love and of divine compassion. This, obviously, is no new message; it acquires its significance chiefly from the unusual experiential circumstances that give rise to it—the state of consciousness associated with the onset of apparent death." In his book, Dr. Ring refers to these near-death episodes as "seed experiences," and in a sense they are no different than the UFO encounters of the third kind that many people have been experiencing in growing numbers, in that they represent not only an actual physical experience for the person involved, but are a symbol to the rest of humankind that it is time our consciousness be expanded into other realms and dimensions...which is, after all, what all our work and writings are about!

Similar research has been conducted by Dr. Michael B. Sabom, Assistant Professor of Medicine, Division of Cardiology at Emory University, and a staff physician at the Atlanta VA Medical Center.

Dr. Sabom began his internship at the University of Florida in July, 1970, and as he had been trained in scientific methodology he was not quick to succumb to talk of life after death, and the supposed experiences of several patients who had reportedly returned from the gates of heaven. But little by little, as he worked with individuals who had undergone extreme heart problems he began to realize that such near-death experiences were more common than he had ever supposed, and seemed to be quite similar in nature no matter who they came from.

Harper & Row published Dr. Sabom's findings in 1981 under the title *Recollections of Death—A Medical Investigation*. In this volume, the author tells of his findings and conclusions based on a personal study of 106 case histories.

"As a physician, I have evaluated the medical circumstances that have surrounded these experiences and have been utterly amazed at the survival of many of these people whose physical condition plainly seemed to rule against their continuing to live. I have been equally fascinated by the descriptions of their journeys while unconscious and near death. My personal reaction to these events is not so much a 'scientifically weighed' response as it is a keenly felt identification with the tears of joy and sorrow that have accompanied the unfolding of many of these stories."

As to what these experiences "mean," Dr. Sabom quotes the words of one of his patients who returned from the dead: "I think it's God's work. That's the only thing I can figure. God had me that time and He could have kept me. From this experience, I know there is a life after death and not just death itself. I think once you've penetrated the big secret just a bit like I did, it's enough to convince you, enough to convince me that I'm going to have no fear...I don't think God wanted me to die...if He wanted me, He would have kept me...He wanted me to get a peek into this big secret and shove me right back again."

Clergyman Explains: "Why I Believe"

And what of the clergy? While life after death may have been an accepted doctrine in decades past, a good number of "modern" theologians subscribe to the theory that when the body dies that's it for all eternity, or at least you're going to remain "in the ground" until the time when Jesus returns and personally lifts our souls up from the grave and either sends them to heaven or straight to hell.

However, little by little, this "dark ages" approach to a very important subject is being radically disputed by men of the cloth who are willing to study all the evidence and make up their own mind based both upon the scriptures of the Bible (which tells us the soul does live on in other dimensions) or by discussing the topic with members of their congregation who might even have been—at least momentarily—closer to God than they've ever been.

One such clergyman is the Rev. R.E. Allten whose writing on the subject of survival became his Master of Sacred Theology thesis to Harvard University. The Rev. Allten originally submitted his thesis to *Chimes*, a now defunct publication which contained frequent accounts of those who had experienced physical death. Rev. Allten's thinking on the topic is clear and concise and is typical of the rationale now being employed by ministers and priests whose bound duty it is to proclaim the existence of God's higher kingdoms.

"It all began on a hot summer afternoon in 1952. I had just served the Sacrament of Holy Communion to Mr. Thurston Wiggin of East Corinth, Maine, who was dying of the dreaded disease, leukemia. Mr. Wiggin had been ill for some time. My predecessor in the Methodist Pastorate at this little rural town in north central Maine had called faithfully at Mr. Wiggin's home for many months in an effort to bring him the comfort of the Christian faith. After my transfer to the parish, I had continued to make frequent visits to the Wiggin home for the purpose of bringing peace of heart and mind to this valiant man who had been putting up such a courageous battle against the onslaughts of the black angel of death. As the months wore on, however, the dying man came to realize that his was a losing battle; he began to reconcile himself to the fact that it would not be too long before the final curtain would ring down upon the last act of his physical life on earth. He requested that I bring the Lord's Supper to his bedside so that he could experience one last hour of fellowship with Christ before the deepening shadows completely closed him off from his awareness of earthly existence. After he had received the bread and wine, he closed his eyes; his head sank back onto the pillow and he breathed a sigh of great relief. His face seemed to be more relaxed and peaceful than I had remembered seeing it in all the time I had been ministering to him. I knew that he had made his peace with God.

"As I rose to make my exit from the sick room, Mr. Wiggin turned his head toward me, opened his eyes, and said in a weak voice, "I don't suppose I'll be here too much longer. My loved ones on the other side were all here last night. They waved to me and said, "Thurston you'll be seeing us again soon. We are coming to take you home. Helen also will be joining us before too long. Fortunately, his wife, Helen, had been out of the room and did not hear the last part of this statement. I quickly leaned over the bed and said to him, 'We hope that you were only dreaming. You'll be around for quite a while yet, so don't take this experience too seriously.' Young pastors, in their zeal to bring immediate comfort, sometimes make brash statements; this was one of my unforgettable false messages of hope. I shall never forget its resultant effect.

"A strange look came over Mr. Wiggin's face as he struggled to frame the words, 'It was no *dream*, Pastor Allten, I was wide awake at the time. I saw those people and they were as *real* as you are. Don't you believe,' he said, 'in angels and in the life beyond the grave." I hastily assured him that I did believe in life eternal," and then sputtered something about remembering him in my prayers. I made a very rapid exit. As I drove back to the parsonage, I thought to myself how unfortunate it was that drugs and opiates had to be used in such quantities to deaden physical pain that the mind became delirious and thought processes distorted. I found a small measure of comfort, however, in the fact that at least the human brain had a way of softening the blow of imminent death, and that God in His mercy had so structured the mind that it was able to cope with any unbearable situation.

"Less than a week later, I committed Thurston Wiggin's physical body to our 'Holy Mother, the earth" in a simple ceremony which was held at the beautiful little Corinthian Cemetery, which overlooks the rolling hills and green pastures of the sleepy little village of East Corinth, where Mr. Wiggin had spent the greater part of his earthly life. His wife, Helen, wept quietly as I intoned the final words of the benediction. She left the grave with the words, 'I'm glad that his suffering is over and that he is now at home with the Lord.' 'Yes,' I thought to myself, 'had he lived on too much longer he might have lost his mind completely; it would have been a horrible thing. As it was, he died quietly with full confidence in a beautiful illusion.' I walked slowly past the graves of those who had been dead for years, stopping only once to look at a gravestone on which was sculptured the image of an angel. I went through the iron gate of the cemetery and back to the land of the living.

"I called on Helen Wiggin two or three times after that. She seemed to be adjusting satisfactorily to her new life. Her grief was intense but she showed every indication of being able to conquer it in the due course of time. She was in good health, had a nice family of grown children, and was qualified to teach school and was thus able to earn a comfortable living. I soon turned my attentions to others who seemed to be in more urgent need of my pastoral services. Life rolled on, as it always does. I moved to another student parish and the Wiggin family passed into the pastoral care of another student shepherd.

"About two years later, Helen Wiggin died on the operating table; she had succumbed to a routine surgical operation from which everyone had expected her to recover. I was stunned when I was informed of her passing. The prophetic words of her dead husband's revelators had come true. 'Helen will be joining us soon,' they had said. Her untimely death seemed to me to be more than a coincidence."

Meeting Your Maker

Lori C. is a spiritually oriented person who has studied UFO literature, Star People concepts, and New Age work in general. She is also an active wife and mother, a happy, cheerful person who practices good metaphysical beliefs in her everyday life, and who makes them work for her both in the daily dimension and in contacting higher levels of consciousness.

Before a near-fatal auto accident, however, Lori was unhappy, unfulfilled....virtually another person according to her friends, and family, as well as in her own conception of her personality.

"I am truly another person," she states. "I remember immediately after the impact, I was laying in this twisted mass of metal which had been my sports car—dying for all intents and purposes...."

Lori shakes her attractive blonde head and tears come to her eyes. "All I felt was utter serenity and peace. Then I began zapping my full power of concentration...my full being, if you will...to a magnificent light in the distance. It was pulsing and shimmering. To go to this beautiful, alive light, I had to sail through a dimly lit tunnel. Its walls were pulsing also, with less-intense energy...as if it was an extension of the focal-point light." At this point, Lori indicates that "light" should truly be spelled with a capital L because this was truly the Cosmic God, the Life-force itself!

"I knew unequivocally and eternally at that very moment that there is life after death! It was as plain as the most simple fact—plainer than ABC had been when I was 6 years old. Death was, as far as I was concerned, only a passageway to a higher level of consciousness! This other level—other world—I saw so briefly was free of all the worries and hassles that we have here on this level. And yet, this level we're on now is a necessary one! Don't make the mistake of thinking that it is inferior or all bad because it is not! We have definite missions to do here—all of us in the human race do—to make this level a better, more Godly place to live!

"So I did see the other side...there is another side...and it is a beautiful place! But then, right as I was sailing through this pulsating tunnel, almost to the Light, I was pulled back very abruptly. I was being put in the ambulance back here. I felt very sad...very sad...to be pulled away from the Light, but I understood that I had work left to do here and that I had not been doing it as I should have been before the accident. I made a vow to the Light and all the beings of the Higher Realms right then and there...to carry forth my earth mission in a more diligent and loving kind of way. I vowed to start by treating my family with the overt love which I felt for them deep inside myself anyway. I just had not been showing it!"

"I became more tolerant, more giving, more unconditionally *loving* not only with my family but with *all* life everywhere."

At this point, Lori's husband chimes in to say that she still seems to him like a totally different person, "Now she is a truly illuminated soul, a light shining for us all, guiding us daily. Before she was petty, grudging, edgy."

Lori laughs lightly and her husband moves over to take her hand, "Oh, I loved her anyway," he smiles, "and I was and am no saint myself. *But* she underwent some wonderful kind of metamorphosis or transformation. I could never say that I'm glad the accident happened, but I do thank my lucky stars and to use Lori's term—I do thank the God-force, that she is who she is today, right now, at this very minute!"

Today Lori does spiritual counseling, helping others to perceive and reach for higher levels of consciousness without them going through a near-death experience. She is devoting full time to her mission and doing it well, making many people "new" again and enthusiastic about life itself. She is so certain about her visit to the world which lies waiting after death that she transfuses this absolute belief and reassurance into other people. We can only say, "Lori, carry on your mission!"

Experiencing a Soul Encounter

When we look at Lori's case with our psychic intuition, we know that she is indeed a blessed and inspired person. She encountered another dimension which touched her profoundly and deeply—right to her soul. In fact, it was her soul itself which experienced and remembers this near-death phenomenon. This is the only way to account for the basic personality change within her! It was not her brain nor her physical body which changed but instead the unique essence which *is* Lori: it was enhanced, energized, re-charged with goodness, before its return to the mundane plane to engage in its life mission. She had been put off her "star path" by several paces, involved in self and negativism. Now Lori truly perceives what life is, how sacred and precious...and how eternal. Lori truly had a *soul encounter* with higher beings!

Lori also states that she feels close to her "special one," a guardian angel. Before the accident, she had barely suspected that such a being might exist, but she had no real communication or contact with this being. However, these days Lori communes with her special spirit guide daily and he gives her strength and assistance in making the right, loving choices and in guiding others. He transmits to Lori the message that *there is no death,* that his soul, her soul—and your soul, dear reader— have been within the Universal Energy for millennia upon millennia. They come from the Universal Energy and they are the Universal Energy! Death in this one lifetime certainly does not mean death of this unique, vital, and ageless energy essence called the soul. It shall never die, only evolve on to brave new worlds, on to breath- taking new dimensions.

More Proof of Heavenly Realms— The White Light and Celestial Music

As fascinating as Lori's experience may be to us, it is within keeping with other similar "after death" episodes that have been reported to us.

Take, for example, the case of attorney Robert D. who should have died during the Second World War, but who is still around today thanks to that "invisible hand" that often saves lives in the nick of time, even when it becomes most unlikely.

"My near death experience happened in 1944 while I was an enlisted bombardier-navigator in a medium bomber group stationed on Sardinia," Robert takes note, going into detail about experiencing the "white light" so many soul travelers have spoken of, as well as hearing strange music which can only be described as purely "celestial."

"My group's mission on the day involved was to bomb a German marshalling area at a small city near the Adriatic, the name of which I can't recall.

"we were told at briefing the importance of the target and that it would be 'flecked up,' a kind of 'last letter home' mission.

"It was a clear summer day with ceiling and visibility unlimited

(CAW weather). This must have been about my 26th or 27th mission although with the lapse of years, I forget that too. It really isn't important, except that it denotes that I had by then, had a good bit of combat experience.

"We turned on an IP (Indicated Point) perhaps 6-5 miles west of the target area, and began flying east. It was about 10:30 or 11 AM and the sun was bright overhead. It was so hot in my 'greenhouse' that I took off my leather flying jacket. In our B-26 aircraft, the bombardier had the best view on the aircraft, as you were out in a plexiglass nose with unobstructed vision.

"As we came closer to the target, I could see flack so thick that the stuff looked like a coal pile, over the city. Earlier medium bomber formations were already bombing the area and as I watched I saw bomber after bomber shot down out there in front of us. By a rough guess I would imagine I was observing a loss ratio of about 65% of the total formations strength.

"It was procedure for the bombardier to keep his intercom on 'local' or within plane during a bomb run, so as to communicate with the pilot and guide the plane right or left as you bombed. Usually the co-pilot kept his radio on command channel so that he could hear the group leader's instructions.

"As I watched the bombers, in the flack being shot down, I suddenly realized that most likely I would be dead in the next few minutes.

"I was then an agnostic. I always said, that if I was about to die I would not get 'foxhole religion.' Recognizing death approaching I still did the automatic things a good bombardier should do on approach. I turned on the intervelometer, armed the bombs and prepared to open bomb bay doors, all the time gritting my 20 year old teeth and saying, 'There is no God and I won't change my belief now.'

"It is taking much longer to type this than the actual time involved. perhaps the whole thing lasted 3 minutes, maybe one. But at any rate, my earphones suddenly were filled with music when previously there had been static. It was indescribably beautiful. You could say it sounded like organs, a full symphony orchestra, violins, or any musical instrument you ever heard. It was almost too low to hear initially but built to a crescendo of sound....something a bit like church music or classical music, but about impossible to describe. And as the music enveloped me, I was conscious of being the center of a very white light. This light, however, gave off no heat and was separate from the sunlight flooding the nacelle. It seems (remembering) that the light extended out from me in any direction 30 to 40 feet.

"I remember thinking, 'So this is how it is to die!' The combination of music and light produced in me a feeling of euphoria absolutely impossible to adequately describe, even though I'm remembering it very clearly some 32 years or so later, and trying my best to be explicit.

"At the time, the music was more enveloping than what I was accustomed to hear from the earphones and radio. As a boy I sat by our church organist as she played, and my skin felt the big vibrations of notes from the pipes. Recalling I think that I was hearing the music and sensing the light from an inner reality, not connected with physical life, because the experience was much more vivid than any externally received music (before or since), no matter whether sitting near a pipe organ, in an orchestra, or listening to my current stereo system at home. (college orchestra 2 years before.)

"And I must emphasize that I *KNEW* I was about to die on that bomb run. It was as if every molecule in my body was boiling with its individual knowledge that the physical entity of me was about to cease except for small slivers of bone, skin, blood to drift down to the ground. In such a heightened state of awareness, just maybe I heard the music and saw the light which may exist in the next dimension(s), because I momentarily 'shifted gears' and could perceive from the 'in' outwardly rather than our customary intake of sensory perception of physical reality.

"The total experience must have been brief. It was over when our formation banked left and turned in a northerly direction to hit a secondary target which proved to be a 'milk run.'

"I called the pilot on intercom and asked why we were banking. He explained that the group commander in our lead plane had decided not to hit the primary, but to go bomb a secondary target to the north (This heard over command channel).

"When we landed, I asked the plot and co-pilot if they had heard the music and seen the light on the initial bomb run. They gave me funny looks and said they hadn't. Afterwards they refused to fly with me, and I was informally grounded in the squadron for about 3 or 4 weeks, with no explanation given.

"After that mission I quit being the squadron agnostic in residence in bull sessions, simply because I concluded I didn't know all there was to know about death and an afterlife, and that God had opened the door to heaven briefly for me.

"That is my psychic experience from WW II. Today, I rarely talk about combat and certainly not that experience. The biggest tragedy of my life (looking back at 53) was 40 missions and a lot of killing of men, women and children. At the time, I was truly a war lover; a volunteer from Tennessee, anxious to go kill Germans. I'm a different person today than that young man in a bomber. This near death episode taught me a lot and changed my life for the better. I'm convinced I was being shown what to expect when I die. I saw the white light and heard the eerie celestial music—I'm convinced heaven must exist!"

The third case we wish to take a look at concerns a man named Lee who had been involved with a life after death experience—not his own—but his brother, Bob's. Unlike Lori, Lee is uneducated, both in book-learning and in metaphysics and spiritualism. Lee is a man of the soil, of the earth. He is a good but simple man, living in rural Tennessee all his life. He has been to Nashville but that is the extent of his travel. However, he is a wise soul and a much-valued life form in the cosmic scheme of things.

No More Physical Pain

Lee watched his brother Bob die slowly of cancer. "It took ten months," sighs Lee, "and it wasn't a pretty thing to watch."

Lee took care of Bob very carefully, helping with all details from personal hygiene to funeral arrangements. The two became even closer than they had been earlier in life; a link was formed psychically.

"Bob told me that if he possibly could, he would get through from heaven—from that other world—and let me know that there is life after death because he thought (and I did, too), that that would be the biggest darn gift he could give me. We thought it was the best 'thanks' in the whole world to just really get the information back through from the other side to the person waiting here on earth. To absolutely have that knowledge…would be the greatest thing!

"Well, Bob died early one Sunday morning, you know. It was raining cats and dogs, very gloomy. I called the parson at the funeral home…there was no one else here and I did the whole thing. I did it even though I was grieving and crying. Bob held my hand as he took his last breath, so I was struggling with that having happened—to actually have been there at the moment—plus all the worries that went with it afterward. Well, I thank you, I had just about had it. That Sunday afternoon, I sat down on the sofa and just started to sob. Neither Bob or I had any other living soul in the universe that we were close to and now I felt that we were parted…that he was as lonely in some cold strange new world as I was here on earth. Suddenly, as I sat there, I stopped my sobbing because a really nice *warm* wave washed over me, almost like being bathed with warm water. I looked over by the fireplace there and I saw Bob. I swear on my life that I really did see him, it was no illusion just because I was so tired!"

Lee continues telling his story with tears welling in his eyes, "You know, it was Bob as he had looked one, maybe two years before his death. He did not have all those horrible things wrong with him that the cancer had done. He looked young and happy and full of joy. He was a whole figure—not just a head or something like in ghost stories—and he was looking right at me! Then, I swear by all that is holy, he nodded his head real strongly—just once—and I knew in my bones that he was saying, 'Yes, there *is* life after death. I am in that heavenly other world and it is just grand here. Just lovely.' Then after that one strong nod as if saying, 'Yep!', he faded out right before my eyes. He just winked out and was gone.

"I swear, I wouldn't believe it if anyone else told me. But this happened to me, doggone it, and I know what I saw and I know what I felt. I also know what I now firmly believe that there *is* life after death in a very good world where there are no wars, no fights, no hatred and meanness!"

After examining Lee's case closely, we find that he and his brother had formed a very real and lasting cosmic bond. Their energies washed together and merged as one consciousness, thus making Bob's visit back from the other world an easier thing to accomplish. In other words, had the two not been so close, Bob might have only been able to appear for a second as a mere blur, but since there was the duality of life energy, Bob was able to appear in full and give a very obvious, concise message.

And we must remember what his message was ...for this is the most important message within the pages of this book: There *Is* Life After Death!

"I Know My Blind Grandmother Can See in the Afterlife"

In the second issue of *Inner Light,* I told a fascinating first person story which is worthy of repeating now since that particular issue was only sent to a limited mailing list in those days.

Christine Colby is a dear friend of mine. For five years we both taught first grade in a St. Petersburg, Florida, elementary school. Chris was always a devoted teacher. She was loving and caring, yet capable of discipline as well as guidance. She has always been a very sensitive and spiritual woman.

Throughout her life, Chris had been exceptionally close to her paternal grandmother. She feels they might even have known each other in a past life. In addition, they were able to communicate with each other even though they might be separated by distance. "When I was sick or distressed, Grandmother Petricelli would call on the phone or arrive at my side without having to be asked," Chris told me. "My Grandmother might have been blind, but her mental capabilities were so keen that they gave her an inner sight which was overwhelmingly beautiful. When Grandmother died, I knew I had not only lost a dear relative, but also a best friend and twin soul."

Chris revealed during the course of one conversation how when her granny died she felt all alone. "It was 1975, I was just 18 years old and had not yet met my husband. I was really devastated. Frankly, while I love my mother a lot, she and I have never had a natural bond nor have we always seen eye to eye on everything. Thus losing my grandmother was like losing a part of my soul.

"Grandmother died early on the morning of August 18th," Chris sighed. "By that night, my parents had taken care of the details of her funeral. My parents, my sister and I were staying at my grandmother's house. We were all physically and emotionally exhausted after a terribly long and hard day. I felt that I should spend the night in Grandmother's room, whereas my sister, who had not been that close to her, said she was too scared to stay in a room where a person had just died.

"I, on the other hand, welcomed this last chance to be near Grandmother if only in spirit. I could still smell the good perfume on the pillow and I appreciated the little belongings that were hers, and had not yet been packed away. I looked at the friendly little room and thought how much Grandmother had hated being blind those five years before her death. She particularly loved nature and bright colors and had often expressed to me how sad she was not to be able to see anymore."

My friend's warm, brown eyes filled with tears as she relived this amazing night. "My sister was teasing me that I should leave the light on all night, that grandmother's ghost might come and haunt me. Actually, I didn't think she was being funny at all. There was nothing for me to be scared of. I had loved my Grandmother. She was a good soul and the darkness in what had been her private place was a very peaceful thing to me. I'm mentioning my sister being a tease to you because it's very important. You see, because of her I'm certain I turned off the lights in that room before I went to sleep. I remember lying there in the darkness, thinking that this was the black world Grandmother had lived in. And yet, I still felt very warm and safe there in her bed.

Eventually, Chris fell asleep in the darkness. "In the middle of the night, when I had been asleep for sometime, I heard someone calling my name. I opened my eyes, and was immediately aware that the light was on in the bedroom. The voice I was hearing was my mother calling to me wanting to know if I was okay, and why didn't I finally turn off the light and go to sleep. I replied that I had been asleep and that I had turned the light off hours ago. My mother could hear that my voice was getting excited, and she came to the door, asking if I'd please let her in. You see, I had locked the door before going to sleep, just to make myself feel secure within my Grandmother's room, and so that my sister wouldn't come back in and tease me.

"The reason my voice was getting so excited was that I absolutely knew why the light was on. I knew that Grandmother had turned the light on in the room! I also understood the message she was trying to get across to me. Her message was that she once again had light, she once again could see...that she was free of the blindness and death that had claimed her.

Chris' account is truly a thrilling one. It not only offers proof that her grandmother's soul survived and that the spirit could communicate with the living person with whom it had felt closest, but that the soul could send back an intelligent, loving message.

Chris' communications with her grandmother continued for a week after her passing. Always the message was clear: "I am alive, I can see, it is very beautiful where I am!"

The final message came a week to the day after her grandmother's death. Chris was shopping in a crowded department store, just leaving the section which displays pocketbooks and purses. At the far end of this large area, Chris' gaze fell on a plain brown purse which was hung against the wall many feet away. There was nothing remarkable about the purse. Nonetheless, she felt compelled to go over to it and turn it around. There, on the other side of the purse was an embroidered petti-point scene of a woodland meadow. Chris' heart thumped with excite-ment and she recalls with joy the feelings that swept over her on this occasion. "That scene was the same exact one Grandmother had embroi-dered for me on a pillow before she went blind. I mean, it was exactly the same! The purse had been accidentally turned to the wall so that the embroidered side could not be seen at all. Still, I was absolutely, and mysteriously, compelled to go way across the room to that plain brown purse and turn it around. In my mind and my soul, I knew that grandma was saying 'Good-bye, I must now go to the peaceful, beautiful land much like this one. I just want to let you know I am alive and joyous beyond words.' After this experience I did not hear from her regularly again and I knew that she had passed on to her lovely new world."

However, Chris did hear from her grandmother on one more occasion...an occasion which was very important in Chris' life.

Chris and her husband had tried hard to have a family, but the doctors told them it would be impossible. Immediately, they started adoption proceedings, but the red tape was frustrating and costly. The wait to get their baby was a long one and Chris became extremely depressed.

"I just sat down one day and cried my eyes out,. she remembers. "I had no one to turn to but my beloved grandmother. So I turned my tear-filled eyes upward and asked her to help me, to give me a sign as to whether we'd get our baby.

"After I had dried my eyes, I felt compelled to go to my jewelry box and there right on the top, was my grandmother's class ring which was very old and very dear to me, but had been lost since before her death. I had been afraid to tell her about this as I didn't want to hurt her feelings. I couldn't believe my eyes as I gazed at that ring because I had looked in my jewelry box many times over the years. There is no way that the ring could have been there all along. It was an absolute miracle and I knew it was Grandmother's way of telling me very soon that I would get my baby."

Sure enough, Chris *did* adopt a child. And so, on that lovely note, my friend's dramatic proof of life after death, draws to a close. There can be no other explanation, for the events that happened to Chris showed that her grandmother truly did conquer death and achieved freedom from physical ailments and emotional worries, transcending to a peaceful and magnificent spiritual meadowland which some of us call Heaven.

Heaven is What You Make It

In my spiritual and psychic education in this lifetime, my guides have shown me that each mind/soul makes its own reality, both while here on earth and also in the afterlife.

Your mind waves are unique unto themselves and they do create the reality which you see around you. Your reality is a hologram created by your mind/soul. Therefore, when you die, you also create the reality to which you will go. Yes, it exists on its own as well...but your mind/soul cannot find its frequency unless it is tuned in (this is like being tuned into a radio station: you simply cannot hear it unless you hit the right spot on the frequency dial!). Therefore, you tune into a reality as you leave this corporeal life. It is basically your choice!

Standing at the Door of Creation

Jesus said, "I stand at the door and knock." He meant that one can find the Christed reality of goodness (heaven) if one is of good heart and soul. You need not have lived a perfect, sinless life, you need only tune into the higher consciousness frequency in order to arrive, upon physical death, at a bright new dimension which can indeed be called the heavenly dimension.

And so, your afterlife stands at the door and knocks. In a very real sense, you may choose a world which is of the Eastern tradition of Nirvana and ecstatic mind experience. Or, your mind may be involved with the pure Christian beliefs, in which case, you can and will find Jesus and the heavenly hosts in all their glory. If you are a starward-bound mind/soul, you will indeed find yourself traveling the stars and exploring new, higher worlds/planets which are now out of your reach.

A Warning

However, if you are obsessed with negativism, with worrying about Satanic influence, with carrying on hatred of your fellow man or of another individual, then your mind/soul is creating even now an afterlife which is not heaven at all. We must not preoccupy ourselves in judging or condemning others for then we do not tend to the beautiful garden of energy which is our own uniqueness, our own soul.

You do choose the world to which you will go...you are choosing it in your everyday actions and deeds even now. You must stay in the positive flow, you must be of goodness and good intent! Have no doubts that there is indeed life after death waiting for your soul, which lives forever.

Reincarnation

In your next life, you may or may not have memories of this life. If you believe in reincarnation, then you will live another life as a human here on earth—or out in the cosmos—for that is the reality you make for your eternal mind/soul. When you do live another life on earth or another planet, if you explore your subconsciousness and your supraconsciousness enough, you will find memories of the life you are living now. It is and will be recorded in your mind-waves for all eternity. The experiences you now have are stored as a computer would store facts…within that unique energy which *is you!* I do not talk here of your brain—for all brains look very similar under a microscope. No, I am speaking of your mind and your soul which are not explorable under a microscope but which are the most precious possessions you own!

The mind/soul points you along your star path of life, it remembers cosmically, it guides with the beautiful God-wisdom which it possesses for it *is* a part of the God-force. It *is* life. It is life eternal!

I cherish each and every one of the thousands of letters I have received which ask about life after death and which *confirm* life after death. The question is every bit as important as the answer…for the question makes the answer a universal truth!

In other words, in reading this book, you, dear reader, are expressing curiosity about life after death. You are opening your mind/soul to the possibility of it and you are beginning to choose what dimensional frequency you want to reach after death of your physical body. In this curiosity you are expressing, you are—at this very second—engineering a bright new heavenly reality for yourself after death. That reality cannot exist unless your mind/soul reaches out to it as it is at this moment. You cannot find the right spot on the dial if you don't first turn the dial! That is exactly the way it is with questions and answers about life after death: Once you start to reach out and to search, you do find the right spot on your dial eventually. However, if you do not make that original move to change the dial, you are stuck on "nonexistence." If you don't question, if you don't reach out, if you become stagnant and non-changing, then you do face the only real death of mind/soul. If you change, reach out, explore…then you live both in this life and in all lives to come. They do lie ahead on your star path, do not doubt this! Life is change. Death is transition. They are one in the same. All is *life*.

When It's Your Turn to Die

Death is a scary subject.

Many of us refuse to discuss our innermost thoughts on the matter even with the ones we love. It is something forbidden, dark, mysterious, and just too plain ugly to be taken seriously—until it is often too late.

How frequently have we seen a loved one near death's door with a lot pressing on their mind, and yet no matter how close we are to that person, we cannot bring ourselves to talk about an issue that is so obviously of immediate importance.

Often in a hospital room or near a sick bed the tension is so thick that you can cut it with a knife.

But why are we so scared as we approach a situation that we must all come to grips with? Naturally, there is much sadness in knowing that a family member, a loved one, or a close friend is not going to be around much longer. However, there's something much more than just sadness that seems to freeze our veins as we find ourselves confronted with the grim reaper face to face.

What we are most afraid of is the great unknown. We are apprehensive about what lives around the next corner.

Luckily there is much we can do to comfort the ill at ease to make the transition a lot more easy on those who are uncomfortable with death.

There are now a handful of organizations that are helping to alleviate the suffering of those who are about to catch their last breath, as well as the loved ones of those who are about to pass over.

One such organization is the Metascience Foundation (Box 747, Franklin, N.C. 28734) headed by George Meek an expert in electronic voice phenomenon and inventor of the Spiritcom, an electronic device described in another chapter which has successfully been used to communicate with departed souls who now reside on other spiritual planes

34

close to the earth's physical surface.

Some of the literature issued by the Metascience Foundation has actually been transmitted across the heavens from spirit beings who once resided right here on our world.

As We See It From Here is one such volume which comes to us via the fate Dr. Jesse Herman Holmes, a leading Quaker who for twenty-five years was head of the Department of Religion and Philosophy at Swarthmore College. Dr. Holmes, who died in 1942, has apparently been lending assistance from the spirit world along with a team of well-known writers, philosophers, artists, theologians and poets, who have "come back" to tell us what it is like on the other side, as well as to assure us that life continues even after we have shed our present shell of a body.

One of the areas Dr. Jesse Herman Holmes and his "spirit staff" seem most interested in is the dignity of death, and ways in which the transition can be made the easiest for everyone concerned.

"There are ways in which people can be helped while still in the physical body," affirms the departed theologian. "Too many times the aged, the infirm, the institutionalized are left alone and struggle to be rid of the physical at the bidding of those energies of light and love which they see about them. Too many leave this world during such struggles. But there are ways that assistance can be given. If those in the older years could have some instruction in the ways of self help, it would be well for them. Unfortunately, society today seems interested only in ways and means pertinent to the material life. Even the churches which many attend throughout their lifetimes, although giving much opportunity for building helpful thought-forms, offer no practical instruction in the ways of leaving (behind) the body."

As We See It From Here continues on by telling the precise way in which the soul departs from the body.

"Ordinarily the spirit withdraws after that period in which the mind turns inward, shutting out the material world. The spirit then begins its withdrawal upward, beginning at the lower extremities. This upward passage is a doubling or condension of those energies of which the human spirit consists. It rolls upward from the lower extremities, and passing through the long length of the body, it enters what was called by the ancients the 'Kingdom of Heaven through the narrow way,'—the small passage at the top of the head which is softer and less dense than other portions of the physical skull. It is the way in which the spirit enters the newly prepared body at the beginning of life. It is the way in which the spirit leaves the aged, infirm and physically insufficient body at the end of life."

The authors find this description extremely fascinating as in several instances that we have personally investigated, those who told about dying described how they felt each and every cell in their body start to go numb and die. The sensation, they told us, started at the tip of their toes and worked their way up the body, until it felt like their brain was about to collapse in on itself.

According to Dr. Holmes (or should we say his spirit), as this transition starts to take place the eyes of the dying roll up and they become sensitive to the energies around them. "The mental screen becomes illuminated at the last breath or two, and the person catches a slight glimpse of surrounding astral areas and the lights. These lights maintain more or less the appearance or form of bodies, hence can be recognized by the departing spirit as those who have gone on or who have been near and dear and who now reside in other dimensions."

As life's last glimmer passes before us, there is, says Dr. Holmes a way in which we can perfect and make easier the passing away of the body.

"When the individual approaching death feels the coldness of lower extremities of the body, he should breathe deeply, evenly, calmly, with the eyes shut and let the consciousness reach upward, feel the upward tug, the tug of the upper levels of the spirit towards the narrow way through which it will escape the body. To be completely relaxed, to breathe deeply, evenly and to resist not the upward tug of the spirit is the way of self-help for the individual. An eager anticipation of this experience with the fire and enthusiasm of ideals is the best self-help that one can have. When one has prepared in this fashion, the demons of fear are exorcised and banished from one's being. There is only love, anticipation, and eagerness to step through the door into other dimensions—a most beautiful experience!"

How to Die

Is there, indeed a *right* or a *wrong* way in which to die?

Probably one of the best papers ever issued on this subject was written by a nurse named Mabel Rowland. It was originally published in 1942 as a 24-page booklet and sold widely for 25¢. The copyright expired recently, and the paper has been kept in circulation by the above mentioned Metascience Foundation. We reprint it here since it is potentially important to all of us who will have to confront death sooner or later.

Regardless of who we are or how we feel about it, each one of us must one day leave the body. But there is absolutely no reason to fear this change, for LIFE is continuous and what is still more comforting, CONSCIOUSNESS and individuality are continuous.

What happens is, that the soul leaves the body we now dwell in, and starts anew in its next phase of existence, vibrating at a different rate.

The change is as natural as breathing and we should be as trusting and fearless concerning it as we are about breathing. There is nothing to fear any more than when we lie down to sleep for the night.

As God's creatures, we are PRIVILEGED to live LIFE and this privilege includes Stewardship of a body! A body housing this dynamic, precious and most wonderful thing in the world—LIFE.

We must take every care of the body, but we are not to presume that we own it. We dwell in it. We do not own it. The Creator put us into these bodies "for the duration" of our earth lives and we are to follow the first law of Nature and strictly observe "self preservation."

We are to fight for our lives to the very last ditch and to protect our bodies to the very best of our ability. Even an insect does as much, instinctively.

Painless as we know "dying" to be, IT is Nature's own process and is arrived at upon the Creator's exact moment scheduled for us in the great plan. When will it be for ME?—Forget it! It is none of our business, but preparing for LIFE afterward, IS.

It is only fair to yourself to take in these few facts which I shall give you, and remember them—you may not believe them—nor do you need to, but it is necessary for you to read and remember them: that is the intelligent thing to do. Then when you need the information it will suddenly pop up out of your sub-conscious mind and be useful.

Now when we have completed this cycle of our earth life and IT is over—finished, we awaken in the next state of our existence, discovering that our thought and feeling reactions are exactly the same as they always were! Remember that. You are YOU. There is no death. There is only a change of apparel so to speak. You have shed the body, but your thoughts and feelings do not undergo any change in the passing out.

However you become quickly conscious of the fact that things OTHER than yourself are slightly, but definitely, different and it is for THAT VERY REASON I am discussing this. So please heed this, that you may not be at all PANICKY, but know exactly what to do.

You probably at sometime have dreamed you were falling. If so you know that the dreamer never hits and hurts himself. He wakes up. In the experience of "dying," sometimes the individual realizes he is going: or he may merely suspect it, but the truth is, that while people rarely admit it, even to themselves, most of them FEAR it.

There is no need to. There is no death: it is a misnomer. The TRUTH is that the actual passing out is not only painless, as I noted a few moments ago, but often beautiful; a NATURAL transition, never to be dreaded.

We do not get whisked to a city with "golden streets" and see angels flying around—No. If there is any such place, which was held out to us as "bait" to be "good" in the theologies we were raised on, then we are certainly not ready, in our present state of being, to take up residence there, anyway.

The REAL of the person leaves the body—very much as a butterfly leaves its old chrysalis. Many, many persons everywhere have seen this passing out. I have seen it myself. Ask any experienced nurse. She will probably tell you of seeing a vaporous cloud of ectoplasm—that's what it looks like to our human vision. It is the silver cord that holds us to our bodies. Everyone has it and here in our earth life it is never severed, but it stretches when we are asleep to let our souls or entities, the real of us, go from the body and experience dreams. Then it shortens again and comes back to the body. It holds "body and soul. together. There might be four or five people present at a bedside when a soul passes out and maybe only one or two of them will have their human vision stepped up to the frequency, even to see this much.

Some of us have seen a great deal more. There IS no death.

Now you understand that you are the same individual after you leave the body as before. No wings, no thrones, no crowns. You may be pleased with conditions, or you may at first be a little disappointed. It just depends on what you have expected.

For the first few days, everyone's fate is the same, whether saint or sinner and after that, there are spheres of life where you will belong...and nothing can keep you out of your sphere. You are drawn into it by the LAW of attraction; that law which proves that like attracts like. We will be with people of the same tastes and degree of spiritual interests as ourselves, just as we naturally gravitate to and choose suitable associates here.

Individual reactions are just that, individual reactions. And there are some people who have lived a sheltered earth-life to a ripe old age, steeped in theological tradition and with fixed ideas about streets of gold, gates of pearl, harps and so forth. These good souls are oftentimes their own worst enemies, being stubbornly unwilling to adjust to anything even similar to their earth life conditions, although the next plane IS similar—surprisingly so.

Some people, through theological training, actually expect, when they realize they have "died" to find the streets made of gold. Certain it is that if they believed that literally while here, they will be of the same opinion still.

Some theologies teach that when we die, the body, soul and entire entity lie in the grave and sleep until the "judgment day." Well, these dear souls actually believe that literally. And when helpers on the other side of life, try to tell them they are the same John or Annie Smith they've always been, but that now their life is going to have a few changes in its working out, they are skeptical and react as they might to a Bunko man at the county fair. Some folks of this persuasion insist on sleeping until "Gabriel" shall blow his horn. They often sleep for years.

Let us consider now, a soul just out of the physical body, through a natural leisurely process. It is YOURSELF perhaps. You are greeting your parents. How wonderful they look and they have been gone for years! They were quite old and a little bent when you last saw them in earth life. It used to grieve and tug at you a little to see them aging and failing. But here they are as lovely looking and as smiling and happy as you remember them when they were young and you were very young, just starting to school back in the little home town.

Perhaps you are dreaming—something like this has happened to you before in dreams. No, they were very brief and fleeting flashes, those dreams, this is real and enduring…Still, your parents aren't saying very much…that is like a dream too. But their gaze is fond and steady and they smile so reassuringly. It is real. And what a nice cool light feeling you have! They embrace you. It is real!

Lovingly, they lead you off into their own circle or vibration, where you will rest and talk. Soon you will experience a lovely drowsy, but very safe feeling, and letting yourself go, will fall into a sleep of anywhere from three days or so to several weeks.

Even the most spiritual personalities we have any record of, remained and rested the first sixty hours or a few days, in the Astral, then sometimes reappeared here on earth, briefly, before ascending into higher realms.

The "dead" person doesn't feel nor act any differently for having "died" but adjustments have to be made, just as they have to be made here on earth. For instance, when summer is waning, we move in off the sleeping porch, wrap up a bit and get out our furs and make a hearth fire...That is all there is to it: it is that simple.

When you have slept for your few days or so after "dying" and wakened to start living in your new environment, you never sleep again. You rest as all do in the spiritual realms, but they do not sleep. The exception is those people I just mentioned, waiting for Gabriel.

Please bear in mind that when the soul leaves the body it doesn't GO anywhere. The change geographically, is no greater than you would experience in life if you walked from one room to another; from a darkened room into a lighted one or from a warm room onto a cool balcony.

Please realize also that while your body is to be protected and cherished, leaving it, in God's own time, is no more to be feared than is sliding out of your overcoat, letting it fall on a chair and walking away from it. And at first there is no consciousness of this "shedding" as it were, of the body of flesh.

Our rate of vibration has changed, that is all. And the life we have entered is so very much like the earth life the new arrival is often quite confused, particularly if he has been taught all his life to expect something different.

Should you ever experience the baffling sensation of walking up to your loved ones, embracing them, while they, completely unaware of your presence, walk THROUGH you, just do not get panicky.

Do the same as you should do in an earth emergency, or any situation which you don't understand. We are told by the Psalmists (Ps. 46:10) to "Be Still." It matters not what your religious belief is, or whether you have any—that is perfect advice. Just be perfectly still, within your own mind and lift your thought to your highest concept— whatever YOU think of as GOD. Call to It or Him or breathe His name silently or aloud, just so it is from the heart, which it will be then—it will be YOU "as a little child" and IMMEDIATELY—even more quickly than I can tell you this, help comes. Pleasant, friendly aid and you are never in that "spot" again.

The helper finds your relatives and loved ones for you. This is necessary when deaths occur accidentally and suddenly. Remember what you are reading PLEASE. Simply raise your consciousness. It is your same old consciousness you know, to YOUR OWN HEAVENLY FATHER. Just say as much as "Father" and help will come. The Astral realm is organized. I repeat: you need not believe this that you are reading, but please remember it. In accidental death and in war time it all happens so suddenly that the soul may be hurtled out of the body and stand amidst a hellish scene of disaster and destruction and see his own body lying there. It isn't a pleasant experience, but it is LIFE. Life is progressive. It blooms and fades and grows again and lifts us from sphere to sphere INDIVIDUALLY and according to each one's consciousness. Stand still and pray. Death is a natural part of life.

If your life here has been devoted to the accumulation of material things or to the making of money, to the extent that you have come to be steeped in it—to enjoy it, say, more than anything else, you are building up a hazard for yourself in the "next world."

Be wise enough not to have your chief interest a material one like collecting or selling to make money, because when we leave the body we go where there is NO ECONOMIC standard—money is not used. You will be a fish out of water unless you have a hobby which is something less material, more intangible and important than buying and selling.

Things "of the earth earthy" are just that. Be careful not to grow so fond of them to be obsessed by them, for once we actually LOVE things or money, then we are in danger of being drawn and held by this earth vibration.

Briefly, that would mean that we should, as a disembodied soul, yours or mine, after we had died, hang around others still in earth-life, whose tastes and activities are the same as ours used to be. Our satisfaction would be merely vicarious...There are hoards of these pitiful earth-bound souls haunting clearing houses, counting houses and money markets and trade centers of all sorts. Also we see the souls morally weak and depraved in drinking joints and low places.

While you are still living your physical existence, realize that money is important to you merely for body-comfort needs. This is temporary, so don't feed your soul to it. In the next plane you see no "business as usual" sign. It is then that your artistic attainments may be enjoyed and you will receive instruction for far more noble service than money grubbing.

So, my advice is, to be prepared...to prepare while still living here. Cultivate your SOUL SIDE. Learn to love and serve your fellow man. If it is not easy for you to love people, it can be an impersonal kind of love until you become a more loving creature. Cut down on the criticisms of others and magnify their desirable qualities. I mean just to yourself, as they start to "irritate" you when you think of them. The way they walk or talk or some little fault. Forget that and refuse to see it. The Hindoo, when he passes another human soul, mutters "pronom," meaning "The God in me salutes the God (part) of you."

I am not being sentimental. I am giving you the key to the situation of living, more fully, both here and now and AFTERWARD!

World wars have come from tiny little warring feelings in the individual HUMAN HEART. People are shocked at first to hear that, but it is true. Self-seeking people here on earth, have competed, connived, monopolized and hated in their driving urge to control. To be top man; to get most; have most; regardless of how and inconsiderate of at whose cost.

Yes, little wars of greed (called "Ambition") starting in the individual human heart, larger wars in families, cities and governments finally form the snowball which becomes a WORLD WAR!

The cure of war is peace and it, also, must start in the individual human heart, with the word "UNITY"...oneness, coming to fruition in deed as well. We are leaves of one tree. Children of the same Father. Coals of one fire. And we are each one endowed with the great solvent power of LOVE, which if recognized and USED, INDIVIDUALLY, would immediately start working to redeem the world.

Let us live with our thought upon God and with this attitude of mind we shall be living the right way—and then surely we will "die" the right way.

Exactly Where Is Heaven?

Heaven is like no place on earth as Dr. Dick, an eminent Scottish philosopher who lived more than a hundred years ago must have realized when he penned the following words:

"Oh, could we wing our way with the swiftness of a seraph, from sun to sun, and from world to world, until we had surveyed all the systems visible to the naked eye, which are only a mere speck in the map of the universe. Could we, at the same time, contemplate the glorious landscapes and scenes of grandeur they exist. Could we also mingle with the pure and exalted intelligences which people those resplendent abodes, and behold their humble and ardent adorations of their Almighty Maker, their benign and condescending deportment toward one another—'each esteeming another better than himself'—and all united in the bonds of the purest affection, without one haughty or discordant feeling—what indignation and astonishment would seize us on our return to this obscure corner of creation."

As we know, the vessel that we call our physical body is very transitory. We do die. The question before us has always been, is the mind and spirit within a person also transitory, or is the thing we call the soul something which retains its life force? And if in fact it does, then where does the mind/spirit find itself after the physical body has ceased to function and is no longer in existence?

In the Christian religion, as well as many other faiths, after a person has died, supposedly, their spirit migrates to a sphere of existence where he or she is either rewarded or punished for deeds performed while on earth. Thus originates the concept of heaven and hell.

Modern Christian theology leads us more and more to believe that the dead are gathering dust and do not live on. Instead they are said to remain in the ground until "Judgment Day" when Jesus—surrounded by an army of angels—will descend from the clouds, slay the wicked, and lift up with Him into heaven those who are worthy. On the other hand, those who have been damned will fall into hell's fiery pit of damnation where they will suffer for all eternity trying to stay out of reach of Satan's razor sharp pitchfork.

Actually, this philosophy is a rather current one which got a foothold sometime during the fourteenth century. It is also *contrary* to what Jesus taught and what the scriptures have to say about the subject of survival.

According to all existing evidence, there is every reason to accept the idea that when we die our soul transports itself to a place, a region, or a level of consciousness that befits the way we lived while on earth.

Heaven, dear friends, is not one single place, but is a series of spiritual zones that are literally the way you believe and wish them to be. There are a multitude of heavens each with their own individual characteristics. In essence, the heaven we go to is a place that is exactly what we deserve, because our minds have created its existence through our deeds and efforts while on the physical plane.

Now don't be quick to call such a belief pure heresy. Before you do, remember that after His resurrection Jesus said that He was going to heaven in order to prepare a place for us, and that in His Father's house there were "*many* mansions." Jesus never said that there was only one heaven. He, in fact, indicated that there were at least several dwelling places where we would go to join the Almighty.

For those needing additional quotes from the Scriptures to justify the thinking of the authors, in the Old Testament Moses told of seeing "The heaven of heavens" (Deut. 10:14) and the writer of Kings 8:27 declared, "Behold! the heaven and heaven of heavens cannot contain thee." The Apostle Paul referred to an experience he had while in the "*third heaven*" where he "heard unspeakable words," (see Cor. 12:2). David, King of Israel, cried out in great ecstasy of spirit, "Praise Him ye heaven of heavens." In Psalm 48:6, he also declared: "By the Word of the Lord the *heavens* were made."

From those who have passed over and returned it has become evident that as a well meaning person you will find heaven to be a beautiful place where goodness and peace abide always.

The material world has its solid walls, streets, trees, etc. and is solid because your mind/spirit has solidified this cosmic hologram due to the fact that the mind must solidify its reality in order to find direction and meaning. Therefore, the dimension of heaven where you will go will be a solid place as well, with walls, streets, trees and so forth. Heaven is literally a higher level of consciousness; a complete and real new dimension for your consciousness to dwell upon.

In order that your soul can reach new heights of awareness, it is very important that you will find your solid and real heaven in exactly the place and within the specific boundaries which you know it to exist. Whatever level of awareness you have progressed to, this is exactly the zone your soul will inhabit in the afterworld.

Briefly, heaven is exactly what you think it is! It will be real and solid for you, in exactly the dimension your spirit perceives and deserves.

Is Heaven a Million Miles Away?

How far away is heaven? Will we have to journey for days in order to reach the promised land? Hardly, for in the twinkling of an eye following your departure from this reality you will find yourself in another dimension surrounded by those loved ones you long to see again, as well as by those who might be called "teachers." These instructors are there to assist you in your transformation and in general to show you around your new home and tell you what to expect.

Recently, we have seen several articles written by clergymen and by scientists conjecturing that heaven may exist on the other side of a black hole in space, or in some other solar system light years away. Such forms of thinking can only originate from those men and women who place reality solely on a physical basis. To their limited minds, heaven must be some place solid. It cannot simply exist here and now, in the etheric. They want to be able to touch heaven, and if they can't touch it then in order for heaven to be real at all it has to be far enough away to be out of immediate range of their scrutiny.

Don't be fooled for a minute. Heaven is right above our heads. It is not some place else. If anything, the truth is that other planets have their own spiritual zones that are populated by a multitude of highly evolved beings, even if we can't see them through the telescope. We know they exist because the Bible tells of such encounters (Ezekiel saw the wheel way up in the middle of the air), and our own files are filled to the brim with the experiences of those truthworthy souls who have found themselves face-to-face with beautiful beings who had a spiritual quality about them that is indicative of the fact that they are far more advanced than we are here on this material plane of earth.

Bet you didn't know either that Winston Churchill was once heard to say that when he died he was planning to go to a place 5,000 miles up. Interestingly enough, high altitude radar has often picked up blips of unknown origin coming from just such an altitude. Such blips have often registered as being upwards of five miles across as if they were some form of "sky island" floating in the upper regions of our atmosphere. Yet, as massive as these blips are, nothing can be seen through a telescope, indicating we are once more dealing with unseen realms or kingdoms.

Here's an even more shocking—and quite titillating—bit of evidence that the spirit world exists nearby. Several times while in the limbo of space our astronauts have heard strange voices coming through their earphones speaking in languages they are not familiar with. On the Apollo 12 mission one of our lunar walkers actually heard the chords of the song "Where Angels Fear to Tread. while he was bouncing about in the free fall gravity of space. NASA also picked up the emission, but they could not trace its origins, and since they were communicating on a special channel with the astronauts, they felt convinced that the song was not being broadcast by anyone on earth. Where, then, was the tune coming from? To our minds this seems to be a way of telling us that the angels of the Lord are always *close* at hand.

Many celebrated individuals—be they well known show business personalities, politicians, public servants and heroes—besides Churchill know the truth about the afterlife, but manage to keep what they know to themselves for fear of reprisal from the organized churches and from spiritually dead society as a whole. They reason that if a person wants to believe there is only one heaven or one hell and that it is a million miles away that's their business. From what we have come to understand, each planet in this solar system (as well as throughout the vast cosmos) is made up of various spiritual planes, the lower ones purely physical in nature and the people residing there materialistic in overall content. This is the type of plane we currently reside on. As we leave the physical by way of the soul, we discover that the planes directly above us are much like the earth, while as we journey higher we come closer to God's kingdom which is of a spiritual and not physical essence. According to researchers, the eleventh plane is the highest, and it is there that you become one with the Almighty, casting aside any remnants of your earthly ways, deeds, or thoughts.

Location of the Summer Land— Over the Highest Mountain Top?

One of the greatest spiritual leaders of our time was Martin Luther

King who did more to spread equality through non-violent means than anyone else we can think of. For all intents and purposes, Rev. King must have had a clairvoyant vision when he declared that he had been to the mountain top and seen the promised land.

A survey by the authors shows that many of those near death report being taken to the highest mountain from where they can see the earth far below and their next home not so far away.

Take the experience of a young boy, who, on his dying bed, and with his last breath, beheld and briefly described the Summer Land.

The little child was dying. His weary limbs were racked with pain no more. The flush was fading from his thin cheeks, and the fever that for many days had been drying up his blood, was now cooling rapidly under the touch of the icy hand that was upon him.

There were sounds of bitter, but suppressed grief in the dim chamber, for the dying lad was very dear to many hearts. Those around him knew that he was departing, and the thought was hard to bear; but they tried to command their feelings, that they might not disturb the last moment of their darling.

The father and mother, and the elderly physician, stood beside the little boy's bed, and watched his heavy breathing. He had been silent for some time, and appeared to sleep. They thought it might be thus that he would pass away, but suddenly his mild blue eyes opened wide and clear, and a beautiful smile broke over his features. He looked upward and forward at first, and then, turning his eyes upon his mother's face, said, in a sweet voice:

"Mother, what is the name of the beautiful country that I saw away beyond the mountains—the high mountains?" "I see nothing my child," said the mother, "there are no mountains in sight of our home."

"Look there, dear mother," said the child, pointing upward, "yonder are the mountains. Can you not see them now?" he asked, in tones of the greatest astonishment, as his mother shook her head.

"They are so near me now—so large and high, and behind them the country looks so beautiful, and the people are so happy—there are no sick children there. Papa, can you not see behind the mountains? Tell me the name of that land!"

The parents glanced at each other, and with united voices, replied:

"The land you see is heaven, is it not, my child?"

"Yes, it is heaven. I thought that must be its name. Oh, let me go—but how shall I cross those mountains? Father, will you not carry me, for they call me from the other side, and I must go."

There was not a dry eye in that room, and upon every heart fell a solemn awe, as if the curtain which concealed its mysteries was about to be withdrawn.

"My son," said the father, "will you stay with us a little while longer? You shall cross the mountains soon, but in stronger arms than mine. Wait, stay with your mother a little longer, see how she weeps at the thought of losing you?"

"Oh, mother, oh, father, do not cry, but come with me and cross the mountains—oh, come!" And thus he entreated, with a strength and earnestness which astonished all those present.

The room was filled with wondering and awe-stricken friends. At length the boy turned to his mother, with a face beaming with rapturous delight, and stretching out his little arms to her for one last embrace, he cried, "Goodbye, mother, I am going, but don't you be afraid—the strong man has come to carry me over the mountains!"

This impressive testimony is based upon the frequently demonstrated fact that the spiritual existence is revealed with all its higher and most beautiful forms of beauty, to the refined and exalted sensibilities of old and young at the solemn moment of death.

I suppose, the idea of a single—all purpose—heaven came about because the clergy found it more difficult to express the afterlife in terms of a variety of places that one can go to when they die. Purgatory, that sort of in-between ground, was the way the Catholic religion handled the problem, realizing that not everyone is all bad, and not everyone is all good. But the idea that saying prayers for the dead will enable them to "move upward" toward heaven is not very likely, since the dead are responsible for themselves, and there is nothing we can do to help them in their soul's journey. The truth is that their loved ones will meet them once they've crossed over and give them advice and assistance so that their spirits may progress.

One man of the cloth who could verify all of this is likely watching over our shoulder as we write these words. Bishop E.W. Parker died in India on June 4, 1901. Before he passed on, he had an experience which shook his soul, an experience which confirms our faith that there is more than one heaven to choose from. The story is told by Bishop Parker's best friend and confidante Bishop Wayne, and is reprinted as follows from the now defunct publication the *Christian Advocate*.

"When I last saw the Bishop, toward the end of January, the previous night he had a vision in which the Saviour appeared to him and gave him the choice of living and suffering or of going to heaven. In the vision he was carried into what he called the *lowest department of heaven* and saw heights and heights of glory above him. Then the Savior said to him: 'These are My little ones who have received Me but have not had much teaching. If you will choose to come with Me I will appoint you to teach these little ones.' As the Bishop told me of this vision he said, 'I have an entirely new idea of heaven. I have a new appointment. I am appointed to continue in service for India and teach Christ's little ones. I am so happy, oh, so happy!"

The Highest Regions

Via out of the body travel, many people have traveled to the spiritual realms with no problem whatsoever. Even one of the authors, Tim Beckley, has undergone a soul journey thanks to the counseling and assistance of Gabriel Green, a Yucca Valley, California New Age worker. Gabe, as his friends call him, has been in the metaphysical field for over three decades. Back in 1964 he even ran for president of the United States as the "space people's candidate. Gabe collected himself over one hundred thousand votes, and many of his platform positions which seemed farfetched then have since been adopted (such as the admission to mainland China into the United Nations). He was also the first to call for global disarmament, realizing fully well that the world was becoming an unsafe place to live in, largely due to all the nuclear weapons being placed into arsenals by many countries.

Through a consciousness rising technique he's developed, Gabe is able to guide those who have a knack for it, to higher realms of spiritual existence. The following is a transcription of the session Timothy Green Beckley had with Gabe Green on Nov. 2, 1982 showing what it's like in the regions a few rungs above the earth plane:

G.G.—From your position out of the body, I want you to go to the fourth plane of consciousness. Stand before your fourth plane consciousness and tell me whether it is male or female.

T.G.B.—I'm stuck in a cloud.

G.G.—O.K. What do you see there?

T.G.B.—How do I get out of the cloud? I see a city there. It looks like the city from *Close Encounters*. I mean it's just like a big city in space. I guess I'm there looking at it.

G.G.—Is this actually a spaceship or a city in another dimension?

T.G.B.—I think it's in another dimension. It's there. It doesn't matter whether it's in this dimension or another dimension. It's there right in front of me.

G.G.—What I mean is, if it's sitting on a cloud or if it is a city or is it a mothership?

T.G.B.—I know what you mean. Let me see…Yes, it's a city. It's a city in the clouds. I don't know if it's an apparatus or a city. It looks like a city to me. There are people walking around and there are plants growing there. It doesn't seem to be like the Enterprise or something like that. It's a city like the Summer Land or something like that.

G.G.—There are these islands floating in space. It's like they are sitting on a cloud.

T.G.B.—Now this isn't out in outer space. It's like in a cloud here in the atmosphere. But yet, I guess it must be invisible to those here on the ground because I don't know of anyone who's seen it. Yes, it's another dimension. Maybe it's what they call heaven. I don't see any archangels with wings playing harps or anything like that.

G.G.—Well, if it's a little higher than here, it would seem relatively heavenly, relative to earth.

T.G.B.—There's a lot of green. I sense a lot of plant life. There are people going about their business like they have work to do. It's not people sitting and meditating like you might expect in heaven.

G.G.—Is there something that you are supposed to look at there or are just passing through?

T.G.B.—I do see something. There is a person there or a deity or an entity. He's beckoning me. I see him surrounded by a tremendous glow or radiance. He says that he is sending me to earth because I have a mission to fulfill. And I'm happy to do whatever I can to help. He says that it's not going to be easy and I don't have to do it if I don't want to. I say no, I want to go. I want to try to help the people if I can.

Apparently, that's what I'm doing now in my own small way. I don't think I was meant to be the president or anything like that. I think I was sent in as a helper. There was a lot that was explained to me then. I see that there are the masters who are helping out with the transition that is going on. Some of these beings, you may think of as spirits, but they seem to be working together, the angels, the masters, and the spirits. They may be working on different levels of consciousness but they seem to have the same program of operation for the planet. They ask permission to send people here. They tell you what you are getting into before you come down, and you get a chance to select the type of environment that you want to reincarnate into. I guess I always want to take the easy way. I don't want to get in too deep over my head and I have got to the point where they allow that.

G.G.—Some choice in the selection of your parents?

T.G.B.—Not as far as individuals go, but only as to the general type of lifestyle; whether you want to be born into a wealthy family, a middle class family, or a poor family. I guess you get Brownie points for the more difficult task. If I had been born into a poor family in some minority group, my consciousness would have been more elevated the next time around. But, I kind of cop out and take the middle road, nothing too difficult, nothing too easy, with a little bit of excitement along the way.

They did tell me then that there was a good chance that this would be the last incarnation, that some of us would permanently be taken off the physical plane. They wanted me to try to explain this to people. It is something which some people have to learn and some people will never learn which is that there is more than meets the eye. There is more than Gabe Green's house here and the rocks outside and the sky and we ought to let people hear about it. Some people know about it and some people don't. Some people have a rough time and some people don't. If Tim Beckley can pull a few people up by the bootstraps and climb the ladder himself and live a fairly decent life, without hurting anyone along the way all the better. We are all supposed to help each other along the way. The message that man has yet to learn is that we are all brothers and sisters under the skin and when you are in spirit, it doesn't matter whether you are rich or poor or black or white or oriental. This is all just a mask that we wear while we're down here. We've got to get over the hurdles and preach brotherhood because that is the cosmic way.

G.G.—Is there something on the eleventh plane of consciousness that would be helpful to look at?

T.G.B.—Am I allowed to look there?

G.G.—Why don't you go up and ask?

T.G.B.—There's a door in my way. It's kind of silly. Should I knock on the door?

G.G.—Yes, sure. Knock on the door. See if anyone will open the door for you.

T.G.B.—I'm trying to knock on the door but my hand goes through it. How do I get around doing that?

G.G.—Ask if it's all right to come in.

T.G.B.—I hear some conversation in the back of the door…They say sure, why not, as long as you don't disturb anything.

G.G.—Let's go to the eleventh plane then and stand before your eleventh plane consciousness. Tell whether it is male or female.

T.G.B.—It's not male or female, Gabe. It's a totally different concept.

G.G.—Do you mean it's both, a combination like an androgenous being?

T.G.B.—I guess that would be the best way to describe it, because it would be a combination of a lot of different elements, the combination of male and female and me and other people as well. It's like a blending of souls. It's like a blending of souls of a lot of people that I love and respect on this plane. I don't quite understand the concept but it is like we were truly one spirit, even though, down here on the physical we are many different souls.

G.G.—The consciousness is so high on that level, that you are all Christed beings; you're sort of one consciousness.

T.G.B.—It's kind of eerie. I sort of have goose bumps thinking about it. I see a giant eye. The eye of humanity is the only way I could think about it. They're telling me to go back, that I will reach this stage some-day but it's not time yet. It's not worth dwelling on what I saw at this point because it's not my stage of development. There aren't that many advanced souls that can relate to that and it's just confusing. On this eleventh plane, which is the plane of the masters really, we are all united together as one soul. Ashtar and I are united together on that plane and he is really me. That's too confusing.

G.G.—No, I understand. If you're all the same consciousness on that level, then for all practical purposes, everyone is everyone else in terms of awareness.

T.G.B.—At this point I am I and we are we and God is us.

G.G.—O.K. Return to the third plane.

T.G.B.—It's like swish, going down a tube or a shaft of light.

No doubt the average reader with little or no background in such matters, will want to know why such information received through extrasensory means should be considered valid. Isn't it possible that such things are illusions or hallucinations?

Of course this possibility always arises, and we ask that caution be our safeguard as with anything we have not experienced ourselves.

"I've worked with several dozen persons to date helping them to raise their consciousness, and it's always pretty much the same story that comes through them about these higher planes, Gabe explains. "I've guided individuals with no knowledge of such matters and they always talk about the heavenly realms in pretty much the same way regardless of their own religious backgrounds." This also holds true with what the authors have uncovered in their own spiritual search for deeper knowledge about the higher spiritual planes of consciousness. On the highest level, we are all one soul united, at peace with the universe, and at home with God.

What more can we say, but that if you feel comfortable with such a revelation feel free to accept it, or if you are so disposed continue to go on in your own spiritual search.

But remember, there are many facets, many levels to heaven. It is as unique as each spirit is unique. Therefore, you can indeed be assured of going to heaven if your soul reaches out to goodness. The sky, the stars, are truly the limit. Your consciousness is free. God has given it the right to choose its dimensions, its own heaven. You may reach as high as you possibly can.

There can be no doubt but that your consciousness (your soul) will continue to progress upward. Not only may you be assured that it will continue, you can know that it will have memory, intelligence, and a sense of direction and being. In short, it will be just as alive and real as it is now in your current physical body.

There is only one true death for the soul and that is stagnation. If you do not try to improve yourself as a human being, if you break the golden rule, if you do not attempt to learn cosmic truths and wisdoms, then how can you expect your spirit to flourish? It is not necessary to know all truths...only to reach out in an attempt to learn some of them...or at least give it a try. In having read this book you have reached out...and will probably continue to do so in many other ways. You are assuring yourself of a "star path" to heaven, a path to a new and higher plane of existence for your soul when this present life is over.

A fiery angelic being as depicted by the late artist Celaya Winkler.

Visiting the Lower Regions

At this juncture, it is perhaps prudent to consider the likelihood of hell. Does Satan's "pit of darkness. actually exist? And if so how do we keep away from its fiery depth?

It is our understanding (based upon the first person testimony of those who have succumbed, if only briefly, to death) that if a person's life has been full of negativity and dread, then when they cross the road to the other side, they are in all likelihood going to find themselves up against that which they have created in their own mind. Jesus once said, "so as a man thinkest, he doest." If a person is full of guilt and his consciousness is not clean, then he will have to suffer the consequences. This is not to say that God is not forgiving, for the Almighty has compassion for all His children, be it a tarnished soul or not. Even the lowest of murderers, rapists, child molesters and cads will get their deserved rewards when it is time to "settle up" with the Lord.

As to whether or not Satan or the devil in a physical form actually exists or not, we doubt it, though the world—and the universe—does have its "darker" side. Since the creation, the forces of evil—otherwise known as the enemies of light—have tried to take control of this planet and put us through a living hell. They have tortured us both mentally and physically with war, disease, economic instability, starvation and a host of other unnecessary plights which mankind could learn to overcome if he could spiritually rise above it all.

Forty-Eight Hours in Hell

George Lennox obviously needed a personal hell in order to rid his soul of the guilt it had obviously collected as a notorious horse thief and murderer of the old west approximately a hundred years ago. Lennox was serving his second term in prison, and as part of his punishment he was put to work in the coal mines during the winter. Quite often he reported that he feared for his safety, but the prison officials ignored his warning and put him back to work far below ground. The convict, obeying, had not continued his work more than an hour when the roof fell in and buried him alive. He remained in this condition for more than two hours. When he was eventually dug out from under this heap of rubbish, the doctors were certain that George Lennox's life was extinct.

He was taken to the top, and on examination by the prison physician was pronounced dead. His remains were carried to the hospital where he was washed and dressed preparatory for interment. His coffin was made and brought into the hospital. The chaplain had arrived to perform the last rites prior to burial.

A couple of prisoners were ordered by the steward to lift the corpse from the boards and carry it across the room and place it in the coffin. They obeyed, one at the head and the other at the feet, and were about halfway across the room when the one who was at the head accidentally stumbled over a cuspidor, lost his balance and dropped the corpse. The head of the man struck the floor, and to the utter surprise and astonishment of all present, a deep groan was heard. Soon the eyes opened, and other appearances of life were manifested.

The physician was immediately sent for, and by the time he arrived some thirty minutes later, the "dead" man called for a cup of water, and was in the act of drinking when the physician arrived.

On examination he was found to have one of his legs broken in two places, and was otherwise bruised. He remained in the hospital some six months, and again went to work. I learned of his experiences while apparently dead, soon after, from a fellow miner and from his own lips received his wonderful story. He is a young man, probably not over thirty years old.

Being a shorthand reporter, I took his story from his dictation. Said he: "I had a feeling all the morning that something terrible was going to happen. I was so uneasy on account of my feelings that I went to my mining boss, Mr. Grason, and told him how I felt, and asked him if he would come and examine my coal room where I was digging coal. He came and seemed to make a thorough examination, and ordered me back to work, saying there was no danger and that he thought I was becoming cranky.

"I returned to my work and had been digging away for something like an hour, when, all of a sudden, it grew dark. Then it seemed as if a great iron door swung open and I passed through it.

"The thought came to my mind that I was dead and in another world. I could see no one nor hear a sound of any kind. For some cause unknown to myself I started to move away from the doorway and had traveled some distance when I came to the banks of a broad river. It was not dark, neither was it light.

"I had not remained on the bank of this river very long until I could hear the sound of oars in the water, and soon a person in a boat rowed up to where I was standing. I was speechless. He looked at me for a moment, and then said he had come for me, and told me to get into the boat and row across to the other side. I obeyed. Not a word was spoken. I longed to ask him who he was and where I was. My tongue seemed to cling to the roof of my mouth. I could not say a word. Finally we reached the opposite shore. I got out of the boat, and the boatman vanished out of sight.

"Thus left alone, I knew not what to do, looking out before me, I saw two roads which led through a dark valley. One of these was a broad road, and seemed to be well traveled. The other was a narrow path that led off in another direction. I instinctively followed the well-beaten road. I had not gone far when it seemed to grow darker. Every now and then, however, a light would flash up from the distance, and in this manner I was lighted on my journey.

"Presently I was met by a being that is utterly impossible to describe. I can only give you a faint idea of his dreadful appearance. He resembled a man somewhat but much larger than any human being I ever saw. He must have been at least ten feet high. He had great wings on his back. He was as black as the coal I had been digging, and in a perfectly nude condition.

"He had a large spear in his hand, the handle of which was fifteen feet in length. His eyes shone like balls of fire. His teeth, white as pearl, seemed fully an inch long. His nose, if you could call it a nose, was very large, board and flat. His hair was very coarse, heavy, and long. His voice sounded more like the growls of a lion in a menagerie than anything I can recall.

"It was during one of these flashes of light that I first saw him. I trembled like an aspen leaf at the first sight. He had his spear raised as if to send it flying through me. I suddenly stopped. With that terrible voice I seemed to hear yet, he bade me to follow him—that he had been sent to guide me on my journey. I followed him. What else could I do?"

"After we had gone some distance a huge mountain seemed to raise up before us. The part facing us seemed perpendicular, just as if a mountain had been cut in two and one part of it had been taken away. On this perpendicular wall I could read distinctly these words, 'This is hell.' My guide approached this perpendicular wall and with his spear handle gave three loud raps. A large massive door swung back and we passed in. I was then conducted on through what appeared to be a passage through this mountain.

"For some time we traveled in Egyptian darkness, I could hear the heavy footfalls of my guide, and thus could follow him. All along the way I could hear deep groans as of someone dying. Further on these groans increased, and I could distinctly hear the cry for water! water! water! Coming down to another gateway and passing through, I could hear, it seemed, a million voices in the distance, and the cry was for water! water!

"Presently another door opened at the knock of my guide, and I found that we had passed through the mountain and now a broad plain lay out before me. Here my guide left me, to direct other lost spirits to the same destination.

"I remained in this open space for a time when a being similar to the first one came to me, but instead of a spear he had a large sword. He came to tell me of my future doom. He spoke with a voice that struck terror to my soul. 'Thou art in hell, said he; for thee all hope is fled. As thou passed through the mountain on thy journey hither, thou didst hear the groans and shrieks of the lost as they called for water to cool their parched tongues. Along that passage there is a door that opens into the lake of fire. This is soon to be thy doom. Before thou are conducted to this place of torment never more to emerge—there is no hope for those who enter there—thou shalt be permitted to remain in this open plain, where it is granted to all the lost to behold what they might have enjoyed, instead of what they must suffer.'

"Far above me and in the distance I saw the beautiful city of which we read in the Bible. How wonderfully beautiful were its walls of jasper. Stretching out and away in the distance, I saw vast plains covered with beautiful flowers. I too, beheld the river of life and the sea of glass. Vast multitudes of angels would pass in and out through the gates of the City, singing, oh, such beautiful songs. Among the number I saw my dear old mother, who had died a few years ago of a broken heart because of my wickedness. She looked toward me and seemed to beckon me to her, but I could not move.

"There appeared to be a great weight upon me that held me down. Now a gentle breeze wafted the fragrance of those flowers to me, and I could now, more plainly than ever, hear the sweet melody of angel voices, and I said, 'Oh, that I might have been one of them.'

"As I was drinking of this cup of bliss it was suddenly dashed from my lips. I was brought back from my happy dreamland by an inmate of my dark abode, who said to me that it was now time to enter upon my future career. He bade me follow him.

"Retracing my steps I again entered the dark passageway, and followed my guide for a time, when we came to a door that opened in the side of the passage, and going along this, we finally found ourselves passing through another door, and I beheld the lake of fire.

"Just before me I could see, as far as the eye could reach, that literal lake of fire and brimstone. Huge billows of fire would roll over each other, and great waves of fiery flame would dash against each other and leap high in the air like the wave of the sea during a violent storm. On the crest of the waves I could see human beings rise, but soon to be carried down again to the lowest depths of the lake of fire. When borne on the crest of these awful billows for a time their pitiful cries for water would be heart-rending. This vast region of fire echoed and echoed with the wails of these lost spirits.

"Presently I turned my eyes to the door through which I had a few moments before entered and I read these awful words: 'This is thy doom, eternity never ends.' Shortly I began to feel the ground give way beneath my feet, and soon found myself sinking down into the lake of fire. An indescribable thirst for water now seized upon me. And calling for water, my eyes opened in the prison hospital.

"I passed through all this, and I am as well satisfied as I am that I am alive, that there is a heaven and there is a hell, and a regular old-fashioned hell, the kind the Bible tells about. But there is one thing certain, I am never going to that place anymore.

"As soon as I opened my eyes in the hospital and found that I was alive and on earth once more, I immediately gave my heart to God, and I am going to live and die a Christian. While the terrible sight of hell can never be banished from my memory, neither can the beautiful things of heaven that I saw."

Hell Fire and Brimstone

Knock on wood, most of us will not find our souls as laden with sin as did poor George Lennox. while we are likely to go through all sorts of personal torment, chances are-we will survive and not have to stoop so low as to murder or rob. But what about those of us—the authors included—who might have committed an occasional sin? Will we have to worry about entertaining the same hellish fate as that no good horse

Artist conception of Heavenly Realm.

The beauty goes on forever—for all of us!

thief whose soul seems to be in such an extraordinary state of turmoil?

We have no reason to believe that this is the case, as very few of us manage to be "perfect" throughout our lives. Let's face it, there are just too many "temptations" glaring us in the eye. And furthermore, except for God, what other person has the right to condemn anyone else for their shortcomings? And just what is sinful and what is not? Certainly to enjoy oneself in a physical way on this, the physical world, is no crime. We should strive to be happy, to be cheerful and to have a good time.

God did not put us here to be miserable, or to kneel in prayer twenty four hours a day. He made this world beautiful so we could enjoy its beauty. He made food taste good so we would eat it. He made sex pleasurable so that lovers could experience bliss. There's absolutely nothing wrong with pleasure. Oppressive religions, political parties, and emotionally unbalanced moralists are the ones who have tried to shackle our minds and hearts for centuries. They have led us to believe that our bodies are ugly and dirty, and that good sensations of any type are against God. This line of thinking, regardless of its origin, is utter hogwash, and unless you can get such guilt trips out of your mind, you might knowingly be creating your own hellish environment in the after-life.

Sex, Drugs and Self-Abuse

During your life if you have been a very materialistic person, who has had problems with sex, drugs, smoking, or drinking, it is very likely that your spirit body will not rise beyond the first rung or two of the heavenly ladder. Not that this is a crime like stealing or murder, but chances are you will feel more at home—and you will be able to work your difficulties out in a more relaxed setting—if you are closer to that which you enjoyed while on earth.

Warning: Sometimes if any of these problems have been excessive, the soul will actually make an attempt to cling to the earth plane, and will try and attach itself to a person still living who is possessed by identical desires. Through this means, a backward spirit can maintain ties with his former "addictions." This is the reason why people are warned not to act carelessly with the occult. Tampering with invisible forces you know nothing about can sometimes turn out to be a frightening experience if one doesn't know how to protect themselves. Mental institutions are filled with people who are not able to shake off entities from the lower spiritual planes. These spirits are trying to make a grab for your body so that they can inhabit it and live vicariously through your vices.

This is the reason that we should know when "enough is enough." Almost anything done short of excess is fine, but the body and mind must never suffer, as such suffering is against God's laws of nature, and thus to be considered extreme self abuse.

Once we realize the situation, we will know what to look for both on this side, as well as the other side of life's curtain. If we find ourselves "trapped" we must find a way on to the next heavenly plane for that is the soul's purpose in existing.

An old fashioned vision of hell. But is it really this way?

Linking Up the Evidence

Is there additional proof, besides the stories of death bed patients, to confirm the existence of an afterlife?

A visual and audio bridge between heaven and the physical world has been manifesting under the guidance of spiritual entities for the past 100 years.

People from all walks of life, some knowingly and others completely unaware of what is taking place through them, have been acting as "agents" to prove the existence of the unseen to a skeptical populace. The methods used by the "other-side" include so called "psychic photography," and drawings, spirit writing and music from other spheres.

Our own work with prominent researchers worldwide has partly been done to prove that we are able to communicate with those who have passed on.

One of the ways in which we have attempted to prove the reality of the hereafter is through the use of a simple device—the camera.

This method of seeing through the veil to the other side was first discovered in Boston in 1862 by William Mumbler an engraver and amateur camera enthusiast. While experimenting with this then unique apparatus, Mumbler was surprised to find when he developed some of his first shots that there were extra faces and forms which appeared on the print. Under close examination he was even more amazed to discover that some of these "extras" were of people that he had known who had passed on.

Other early photographers who found their photographic plates "ruined" with images of people who were not meant to be there included Frederick Hudson and French medium Eugene Buguct. Attempts to prove these photo images the work of hoaxers was difficult. Many of the early researchers were out to prove fraud in any way possible, thus they conducted experiments with psychic photography under what they thought were the tightest of conditions. But photography was in its infancy and since most researchers were unfamiliar with trick techniques it is possible, that many frauds were perpetrated.

In 1971, a freelance photographer was on assignment in Central Park to photograph a group of young actors and actresses who were rehearsing for an upcoming performance. Among those there that day was a girl who had appeared in two of filmmaker Andy Warhol's movies.

The photographer took three rolls of film, developing them all the same evening. She printed only those she felt showed the performers at their best. As she went back over the proof sheets a second time she was puzzled by a cloud-like vapor over the girl's face which showed up only on one negative. She knew that it could not be a faulty print or an accidental image added in the dark room by herself.

Blowing up the negative she saw even clearer what had only been barely visible on the smaller print. The girl's face was enveloped partly by a fluffy form which had not been visible to any of the others in the park. The camera had captured something the human eye could not see. But what? And why?

When the photographer showed me what she had picked up on the film I immediately recalled seeing photos of ectoplasm taken during seances held in darkened rooms with infrared film. In many of the cases the ectoplasm was emanating from the mouths of mediums and on several occasions supported levitating trumpets. Barbara had obviously caught this phenomena with her camera, and in daylight at that?

As unusual as it might seem, the professional shutterbug has managed to cross over to the spirit planes several times, but let her good friend the well known psychic Shawn Robbins continue the story.

"I had been booked to appear several weeks later to do psychic readings for a group of businessmen at a Manhattan hotel. Among those who I gave readings to were lawyers, airline pilots, doctors and owners of large corporations. Many of their wives were among those who eagerly waited in line for as much as an hour to talk to me.

"The photographer wanted to accompany us hoping that she could reproduce the strange spirit effect once again. I explained that such shots were a one in a million chance. But in spiritual phenomena there is no such thing as odds—for once again her camera caught what no eye could see.

"On several frames the faces of those present are distorted and rays of light streak haphazardly across the film. Experts have looked at the pictures and have declared them truly unique. One explanation offered is that she might have jerked her camera causing everything to "jump."

However, they also admit that if this were the case everything else in the picture would be blurred—this did not happen!

"Thankful for her uncanny ability to capture true spirit forces on film, I sometime later invited her to attend a seance. We were all seated around in a circle, holding hands and concentrating on making contact with any spirits who might have been in the room. All during the seance Miss Seiler snapped away unaware of what her camera lenses were picking up in the almost totally dark surroundings. When she returned to her darkroom to develop the prints she found this time a series of streaks projecting from the area around my head. Apparently, while in a trance my body had given off psychic energies which showed up on photographic paper."

The question arises, why is this free lance photographer able to get such remarkable photographs when other photographers fail? There is a strong possibility that she is acting as a focal point herself, creating at least part of the energy necessary to produce these manifestations.

Dozens of authentic photographs taken by other photographers do exist of course. In her book *Master Guide to Ectoplasm,* Harriet Hoswell says that the best psychic photo she has ever seen is owned by a Dr. Pierette Austin. It shows an amputee seated in the front row attending a lecture. The man's leg is missing, but in the second photo of the series the "etheric" outline of the man's leg is clearly visible—but casting no shadow, as does the other leg.

At a seance in Philadelphia the sitters saw weird light bands flickering throughout the room. When photos were developed, all of which were taken in complete blackness they showed a semi-round ball of light which had left its mark upon the photographic paper.

Photos taken of a medium from Brooklyn show weird light flashes up and down the right and left hand portion of the photographs. It is almost as if "spirit fireflies" were in the atmosphere. Again nothing was visible to either the photographer, the medium or anyone else. One photographer I showed these photos to suggested the effect might have been caused by static electricity. A second professional discounted this explanation by saying that static electricity did not produce this type of effect.

"Thoughtography has been produced in abundance by individuals who are usually seated in a chair, after having been told to relax and then given a Polaroid camera. Concentrating on a loved one who has passed on they hold the camera in their hands, aim it at their forehead and snap the shutter. In hundreds of cases familiar faces appear on the finished film as if the "dead" had projected them there. In some instances scenes of unknown locations have shown up on the developed prints. Under any of these circumstances strange figures, forms, structures and events have shown up—again with no sound scientific explanation.

Why is the camera able to capture what the human eye cannot see? According to experts, photographic emulsion is very sensitive and is able to record things in a range far above and below what the eye sees. Also the silver solution in the developer picks up electrical particles which might have been in the air—and since the psychic forces are partly electrical in nature it picks them up in all their glory. In addition, when taking spirit photos the shutter speed should be very slow. This leaves the lens open long enough to capture any stray elements floating in the atmosphere.

Trance Drawings and Spirit Artwork

Victorien Sardou was born in Paris in 1831 and died there in 1908. During his life Sardou was responsible for nursing early French psychism and was an accomplished medium who is said to have been able to move heavy wooden objects across entire rooms.

One of his spirit guides is reputed to have been Bernard Palissy a potter who in the mid 1500s produced decorative pottery. Each morning Palissy is said to have taken control of Victorien Sardou's arm and through him produced a good number of drawings and paintings which later sold as rather expensive collector's items.

Kahil Gibran author of *The Prophet* was a combination mystical poet, philosopher and artist. He believed that art was the "universal language" and drew on his contact with the collective unconsciousness for inspiration. Many of his paintings are vivid examples of spirit art.

Another Frenchman by name of Augustin Lesage (1876–1954) had his life drastically altered when he heard a voice tell him while working as a miner hundreds of feet below the surface that "one day you will be a great painter."

One of his truly great performances was revealed in a piece called "The Egyptian Harvest." In this work, Lesage painted a section which is identical to part of a painting existing on the wall in the Tomb of Mena in one of the Pyramids. There is no way that Augustin Lesage could have seen the inside of this tomb—he must have been helped by someone who had been there, and is now residing on a spiritual plane.

In Baltimore's Johns Hopkins University stands a mural covering two entire floors. Painted by Robert Hieronimus it is the symbolic creation of the earth from its beginning on Atlantis to its prophetic inter-pretation of the future of the planet and the rising of this continent.

Scattered throughout are UFOs from other worlds, mystical ser-pents, Biblical references, etc. Hieronimus is an adept who teaches classes in various occult topics at the Aquarian University which he hopes will be accredited by the state of Maryland shortly.

Cosette Willoughby is an inspirational artist whose drawings are reminiscent of faces brought over from the other side in spirit photogra-phy. She recently discovered this unusual gift." I purchased a pack of 3x5 file cards and a typewriter eraser, the kind you can sharpen like a pencil. I took one of the cards and covered it with the lead from a soft pencil point. Then I dampened my finger in my mouth and smeared the lead. From nowhere faces began to appear. I then took the eraser and went over the card bringing out the faces more clearly."

Mrs. Willoughby believes that anyone can produce the same effect by following the method which she used. "Once you start making these pictures you won't want to stop for each one is so different and some of them are really art of the kind produced by the masters."

Cosette mentions that your thoughts and moods have a great influ-ence in what comes out on the cards. Her best results were received in a haunted house. She mentions that she is not so much interested in what appears but rather what is causing her to channel her energies in this direction. Perhaps we can all benefit by learning more about this.

Spirit Writing

More than 14 years before the actual sinking of the Titanic a writer by the name of Morgan Robertson published a book, the plot of which surrounded the fate of a passenger ship on its maiden voyage overseas. In a dream Robertson saw flags flying and bands playing at the moment the ship was struck from behind by an iceberg. "It was certainly the most imposing ship I have ever seen," he stated. Although everyone was happy he could feel some tragedy in the air. "I knew I should warn someone but how could I when it was only a dream?"

So he did the next best thing—he made an outline of the dream and in two months finished writing a book that he sold to a Boston pub-lisher.

It sold so poorly that the book, published under the title, *Futility* was soon forgotten by everyone—except its author who realized 14 years later that he had had more than a dream. His book serves as doc-umented proof that man can see into the future.

Other great works have been produced with guidance from heaven. In the early 1880s a New York dentist by the name of John Ballou Newbrough began writing under the direction of invisible "callers" a book of some 926 pages. Called *Oahspe* it contained more than a million words and was written at the rate of 120 words per minute a miracle in itself on an 1880 Sholes typewriter. Much of the material in this book has recently been "discovered" by scientists and deals with such complex topics as space travel, engineering, etc. No mortal man could have known these things!

Music Composed by Spirits

Relatively untrained in playing music, Mrs. Brown has appeared in front of people like Leonard Bernstein who could find no indication of fraud. These famous composers guide her hands to play and write in manuscript form music far beyond her own skills. World famed composer, Richard Rodney Bennett claims that her talent is absolutely remarkable. "I've no doubt she's psychic. She's told me things about myself she just couldn't have known about otherwise. I was having trouble with a piece of music and she passed along Debussy's recommendation—which worked. A lot of people can improvise but you couldn't fake music like this without years of training. I couldn't have faked some of the Beethoven myself."

Franz Liszt was the first artist to come to her and stand by the piano and actually guide her hands over the keys. All the other names mentioned come in the same way and her vivid description of their appearance gives additional credence to her explanation of how this music has arrived.

The authors have given the reader various solid examples of how the spirit world is able to communicate their existence to us. When we have come to accept the reality of these other realms, we will find our world a much better place. Spirits have much to offer us in the way of assistance and ask nothing in return except an open mind and a kind heart. We have nothing to lose, and much to gain by our link with the next world.

A futuristic look at the world we could likely visit after death.

Can the Dead Pick Up the Telephone and Call the Living?

The title of this chapter may sound like it's asking an absurd question, but the answer is not as obvious as you might think.

Parapsychologists (those scientifically trained individuals who study life after death and the question of the soul's survival) have now documented dozens of cases in which those who should not have been able to, have communicated across the borders of life to those who can still answer the phone.

Ida Lupino is one of Hollywood's legends. Her show business career spans several decades. In fact, show business has always been in Ida's blood, as her parents were always involved in the performing arts.

So much so it seems that often as a young girl Ida was left behind with her grandmother in London while her folks toured on both sides of the Atlantic.

One evening when she was nine, Ida found herself in a fitful sleep. She woke up sometime before midnight thinking about a good friend of the family. She saw that he was seriously ill in her nightmare, so she ran downstairs to tell her grandmother about the content of her dream.

Once downstairs the phone in her grandmother's flat started to ring and since her grandma was busy in the kitchen Ida ran to pick up the receiver.

According to Ida's story which was related first hand to journalist Danton Walker, the voice on the other end of the line seemed far away, but clear enough for her to tell that it belonged to Uncle Andy, the friend of the family she had just been dreaming about.

"The voice became stronger and I could understand the message which was repeated monotonously several times: 'I must speak to Stanley. It is terribly important.'"

Ida turned the receiver over to her grandmother who also recognized the voice as that of Andy. "Whatever is the matter?" she proclaimed upon hearing his obviously troubled speech pattern. "I'll tell my husband you called the minute he walks in."

Right in the middle of the conversation the phone line went dead. The switchboard operator at the residence where they lived was rung up and she went so far as to deny that any outside calls had been transferred to their apartment that evening.

Upon his arrival home, Stanley was given Uncle Andy's urgent message. Immediately, his face became pale and he fell into the nearest chair. Shaking, he informed those present that it must have been someone else on the phone, because Andrew Meyer, the friend in question, had died three days earlier, upon hanging himself!

As eerie and "out of place" with reality as this account may seem, it is by no means that unusual for the dead to be able to telephone the living. Two well known parapsychologists have, in fact, documented several dozen cases of this very nature. *Phone Calls from the Dead* (Prentice Hall) by D. Scott Rogo and Raymond Bayless is an extremely fascinating volume which goes into such cases in extreme detail.

In chapter two of their book, the authors tell how they had spoken with a woman, a Hollywood actress, who was involved in such a "phone call" back in Texas when she was eight years of age.

"My mother had a very dear friend whose daughter had gone away to college. The daughter came back home around the first of the year, each year. The third year, while on her way back home, she was killed in an automobile accident.

"A couple of years later we were over at the home of this friend of my mother's for Thanksgiving, which was one of the holidays for which the daughter used to come home. The telephone rang. I was at the age when the grownups were away in the living room, and the kids were always running around. I would answer the phone. I picked it up and heard the long-distance operator say, 'I have a collect call.' She mentioned the name of my mother's friend and she mentioned the name of the daughter. This threw me a little bit even as a child, and I said, 'Just a minute.' I went and got my mother's friend. She came to the phone. I stood watching her, because I had heard the name and thought that maybe somebody was playing a joke on me or something. She listened to the phone, turned absolutely white, and fainted."

When the woman came to, the oldsters in the group huddled around her to find out what had brought on her condition. The woman was nearly speechless. Finally she said that she had heard the voice of her deceased daughter and that the girl had said "Mommie, it's me. I need twenty dollars to get home."

Scott and Bayless explain further that before leaving school the dead teenager always phoned home and asked her mother to send her money as she considered this good luck.

Once again, as in many similar episodes, the long distance operator was rung up but no trace of such a call having been placed was ever found.

The question arises as to how we might go about explaining such a phenomenon—as a person receiving a telephone call from the dearly departed. Quantum physics tells us that ours is a multi-dimensional universe. An infinite number of dimensions cross through each intersect point which composes this dimension. Therefore, as the soul is freed from the body upon death, it merely tunes into one of these many worlds. The world which it is tuned into is of higher consciousness if the soul in transition is of basic goodness and flexibility. And what ties these multi-dimensions together? Science tells us that the molecular density of a dimension is tied together by electrical energy charges. These energy charges bind these various dimensions together as well as act as the borderland between them all.

On what, we might inquire, is the telephone run? It runs on electrical energy charges as well. Did you know, that when you pick up the phone and dial and when somebody answers on the opposite end of the line, they are not really listening to your voice as you have transmitted it? Instead, they are listening to molecules that have been broken up at one end of the line and reassembled at the other end, thanks to the use of a minute electrical charge.

Edison's Dead Man's Gramophone

Sure, you know who Thomas Alva Edison was—what American wouldn't? But you're not likely to know that outside of perfecting the electric light and inventing the gramophone, the most respected genius of our century also had his bizarre side. According to recently uncovered personal papers, Thomas Edison held a strong belief in several aspects of the occult. He accepted as fact the theory of reincarnation, befriended a controversial medium whom he had engaged in telepathic experiments with, and took life after death so much for granted that he actually had diagrams drawn up for a machine he said would enable each and everyone of us to talk to deceased friends.

Like many inventors, Edison was not overly anxious about taking credit for his brain storms. He felt that much of what he put down on paper for the benefit of mankind, originated from a "higher source," and that he was simply a vehicle or "channel" through which this information could flow freely. It is said that he would hold up for hours in his private laboratory refusing to see anyone even if they had an appointment. Edison would sit by his desk, his eyes half closed, busy scribbling all sorts of notes and formulas as if he were in "another world." Parapsychologists who have had the opportunity to examine his original papers, feel strongly that much of his work resembles "automatic writing," believed to be transmitted from the spirit plane.

As outlandish as such a theory may seem, there is ample proof that it is based upon the truth. For one thing, Edison greatly admired Helena Petrovna Blavatsky. Best known as Mme. Blavatsky or H.P.B. for short, this rather stocky, woman of Russian descent, founded Theosophy of which Edison was a member. Among the beliefs of this religious/mystical order was that a super "root race" had once lived on the lost continent of Atlantis, and that the "Masters of Wisdom" guide and inspire us from another realm. Edison was quick to quote from Mme. Blavatsky's 1200 page opus, *Isis Unveiled*, which contains all sorts of strange occult tidbits. This volume was said to be Edison's most prized possession, and he referred to it often for inspiration.

Being a member of the Theosophy movement (which attracted upwards of a half million followers at its peak, and is still active today), Edison held a strong belief in reincarnation. He didn't see where it was likely that God would have created a soul only to destroy it after a few, brief, years on earth. Edison's library was stacked with reference works on the subject of rebirth. (One book in particular, *The Finest Story in the World,* by Rudyard Kipling, gave Edison a bigger charge than we might get out of watching Seka or Marilyn Chambers going through their pornographic paces on our home video, for the British author's work dealt with a London bank clerk who is allowed a glimpse of a former life as a Greek galley slave.)

Indeed, Edison could be most philosophical when he wanted to be, though there are some who are likely to say that he was crazier than the Mad Hatter when it came to speaking his mind on matters of religion and survival after death.

"The soul of man is composed of swarms of billions of highly charged entities which live in the cells. I believe that when a man dies, this swarm deserts the body, and goes into space, but keeps on and enters another cycle of life and is immortal." Edison held this position and was not ashamed to talk to the press about such matters, despite the fact that they were more anxious to know about his latest invention, than his way out theories on subjects which it might have generally been felt only the insane speculated about.

After his own death, this peculiar—and highly enlightening passage—was found in Edison's personal diary. Perhaps, more than any other statement, this quote best illustrates his fascination with the unknown: "I cannot believe for a moment that life in the first instance originated on this insignificant little ball which we call the earth. The particles which combined to evolve living creatures on this planet of ours, probably came from some other body elsewhere in the universe." If Edison were alive today, he no doubt would accept as real UFOs and would likely have invented a device to communicate with the occupants of these silvery disks so many have seen. In fact, if you read between the lines of his most intimate, personal, thoughts, you begin to wonder if Edison didn't consider it within the realm of possibility that we might all be "space travelers," destined to live out our future lives on other worlds in space. "Take our own bodies," Edison explained, "I believe they are composed of myriads and myriads of infinitesimally small individuals, each in itself a unit of life, and that these units work in squads—or swarms, as I prefer to call them—and that these infinitesimally small units live forever. When we 'die' these swarms of units, like swarms of bees, so to speak, betake themselves *elsewhere,* and go on functioning in some other form of environment."

In all actuality, no matter how far fetched his thoughts became, Edison always thought it best to speak his mind. History shows (despite the fact that it tries to make *light* of the fact), that Edison was often a champion of controversial causes, especially where the occult and psychic phenomena was concerned.

For instance, during the most successful years of his career, Edison befriended an elderly Jew who many thought rightfully belonged in the pokey.

Born in Posen, Poland, Bert Reese had gained a considerable reputation as a clairvoyant. It was said that he could "read minds," and when the vibes were right, actually see the future. Reese had had a number of minor brushes with the law. These had come about mainly due to his methods of giving tips on the stock market and trying to get the wealthy to invest in a number of his schemes which included a supposedly perpetual motion machine. However, this did not stop Edison from taking the elderly immigrant seriously. Not one to have his feathers ruffled by public sentiment, Edison conducted several successful experiments with Bert Reese.

"I asked Reese to arrive at my office at a specific time. I did not tell him beforehand what I was planning to do," Edison went into considerable detail in his diary to describe the nature of his "fool proof" test.

"After he had arrived, I called in a workman whom Reese had never met before. I asked the man to go into a nearby room and to take a piece of paper and upon the paper write the name of his mother, where she was born, as well as the answers to several personal questions.

"The workman followed my instructions to the letter. There could have been no way for Reese to know what the man had written down, but he did! He gave all the correct answers, and, in addition, told me how much money the workman had in his pocket."

But, still, Edison wanted to do more to test this man's powers. Leaving his laboratory he walked to another building and with a pencil wrote: "Is there anything better than hydroxid of nickel for an alkaline battery?" The moment Edison reentered the room where the clairvoyant was he got his answer: "No, Mr. Edison, there is nothing better than hydroxid of nickel for an alkaline battery."

Edison was dumb-founded. The electrical wizard and the psychic soon began to spend more time together developing a rather close—and profound—friendship. Edison seemed very interested in showing off his oddball, human discovery. He would frequently hold small gatherings in his laboratory at which time Reese would be asked to "perform." It is said that many scientists, and men of letters, attended these meetings which Edison described as "seances." Usually, these guests would go away scratching their head in wonderment, so amazed were they at what they observed happening. On one occasion, Reese described to Dr. James Hanna Thompson, a well known alienist, the contents of his roll top desk down to the smallest item in a hidden compartment inside one of the drawers. From several of Dr. Thompson's private papers, he wrote down words which he could not even pronounce, words which had special meaning to the doctor.

Unfortunately, Bert Reese got caught up in criminal proceedings when he began to inform the heads of large corporations where they might find fraudulent entries in their ledgers. The police thought he might somehow be involved and he was brought before a New York judge. Just as it appeared he might have the book thrown at him, the controversial seer told the judge how much money he had in a certain bank, as well as the contents of a sealed letter the judge had in his private chambers. The case was quickly dismissed.

Said Edison of mental telepathy, ESP and Bert Reese: "I tried to undertake a series of experiments to attempt to transfer the thought of one person to another by all sorts of means, but without results. Also I tried to solve the phenomenon by the help of an electric apparatus fastened to the head of the operators. Four among us first stayed in different rooms, joined by the electrical system of which I have just spoken.

"Afterwards, we sat in the four corners of the same room, gradually bringing our chairs closer together toward the center of the room, until our knees touched, but for all that we obtained no results. But Reese has no need for any apparatus or any special condition in order to function. I do not pretend to be able to explain his faculty. I am convinced that the needs of civilization will produce some great discovery by means of men endowed with this power. The rare seers of this generation will become the multitude of the next generation."

It is probably because of psychic Bert Reese that Thomas Edison tried to invent a device which he was convinced would change the entire world. From the above quoted passages it's obvious that Edison held to the idea that a machine might be built which could actually replace the medium in the seance room. He told only his closest friends about this project, and best that he should, because they were even stunned to learn that their associate had formulated a plan to build a "dead man's gramophone."

"I've never seen Edison more serious in all the years we've been acquainted," reflected a local politician who knew him quite well. "He was literally obsessed with the belief that a device could be built to talk with those who had already passed on. Edison thought it would be the greatest scientific invention of all time."

During the period of six or seven months, Edison worked full time on his dead man's gramophone, he wouldn't let anyone come near his office. Only the cleaning woman was allowed inside, and she later reported that his lab was a mess of wires and dials and panels. "I proclaim that it is possible to construct an apparatus which will be so delicate, that if there are personalities in another existence or sphere who wish to get in touch with us this apparatus will give them the opportunity. Why should personalities in another existence spend their time working a triangular piece of wood over a board with lettering on it when something much better can de devised?"

Nobody knows why, but Edison never released his strange communications device. His invention, if it was ever completed, appears to have died with him. There are those, however, who claim that Edison's greatest invention of all time was suppressed, and that he was repeatedly warned that such an invention would cause utter havoc and might bring about society's fall. It was theorized that religious leaders wanted Edison to give up working on this device, and put pressure on him not to release his findings to the world.

So far only random scattered notes have been unearthed, and so perhaps Edison took what he knew about the afterlife to the grave with him. And while we remember him best for inventing the modern light bulb and laying the ground work for our most advanced recording devices, Thomas Alva Edison's greatest contribution to mankind may still be forthcoming—a machine which will enable us to talk to the dead!

Electronic Voice Phenomenon

And even though Edison may not quite have mastered the means of inventing an electronic device to talk with the spirit world, others just as wise, have followed closely in his footsteps, and may have managed to take several giant leaps forward for mankind in the last few decades with a device which most of us take for granted—an ordinary tape recorder.

It all started in Germany when a man attempted to play back tapes he had made of rare birds chirping in the woods near his home. Upon playing back the tapes he was able to make out in the distance voices which he had not heard upon making the tapes. The voices seemed to be human, and they appeared to be calling his name. Listening more closely the man was shocked to discover that one of the voices sounded exactly like that of a close friend—a business associate who had died two or three years prior to his historic walk in the woods. He was stunned (to say the least), but repeated experiments brought identical results and thus the new science of "electronic voice phenomenon" was born.

Today, an estimated two hundred parapsychologists in fifteen countries have had positive results when attempting to record the voices of the dead. Respected author and psychic researcher Harold Sherman has listened to hundreds of spirit voices on tape and is convinced they are legitimate and not hoaxes. One organization operating out of a small office in Severns Park, Maryland has a file of over 20,000 tapes of this type. Sarah Wilson Estep, who probes this enigma says that many of the voices tell of a life everlasting and of peace and tranquility not to be found in our physical dimension. The voices, also say that there is much to learn where they are, and that the afterlife is a vast place, very pretty and very bright.

The Work of Dr. Mueller and George Meek

What Edison might have failed at, a North Carolina man by the name of George Meek may have finally perfected.

Working in conjunction with a psychic inventor named William O'Neil, "Spiricom" has successfully been in operation for several years. Used as an "intercom" between spirit planes, this ham radio-like device was actually developed with the help of scientists who no longer number among the living.

The Metascience Foundation of Franklin, N.C. is the brainchild of electrical wizard George Meek who because of personal evidence believed it was possible to communicate on a regular basis with the so-called dead. He was helped along in his work by O'Neil who professed to be clairvoyant, but once they got started on their project they found out that inventors on the "other side" were willing and actually *anxious* to lend a hand to perfect such a machine.

After much labor, "Spiricom" has become a reality, thanks mainly to the assistance of a deceased physicist, Dr. George Mueller, who helped to iron out the bugs that at first existed in building such a two-way radio between our world and the next

When Dr. Mueller initially started speaking over Spiricom those operating the apparatus had no knowledge of who he was. It was only after they asked him repeated questions that his background began to emerge. They checked existing records in other states, and found that a Dr. George Mueller had indeed once lived and had taught at Orange College in Costa Mesa, Calif. Other claims that Dr. Mueller made from the beyond were all proven to be a hundred percent accurate. When asked to help in perfecting the Spiricom he agreed, and little by little the quality of the voice transmission began to improve and the messages themselves became of greater length and of more scientific and philosophical importance.

Indeed, listeners can hear Dr. Mueller's conversations for themselves, as some of the most important transmissions have now been made available to the public. Interested parties can contact Metascience directly at Box 747 in Franklin, N.C. 28734.

A Personal Performance

With the widespread use of the telephone answering machine, it is possible that many of you reading, this book will actually—sometime during your life—record for posterity a message from a friendly spirit.

Just recently, shortly before work was completed on this manuscript, one of the authors (Tim Beckley) played a tape of a spirit voice which came through to the living in just such a fashion.

Jimmy (not his real name) had attended a spirit circle for the express purpose of asking questions of a deceased friend who had not long ago made the transition to another reality. His friend came in "loud and clear" for more than ten minutes, rattling off descriptions of the kingdom he now occupied. Just before "signing off" Jimmy's friend announced, "I will speak to you again soon," in his normal tone of voice.

A week or so later, Jimmy returned home from work and proceeded to play back the messages on his telephone answering machine. On the tape was the unmistakable voice of his deceased friend saying, "I promised I would speak to you again soon." Then came silence.

So before you run down to the nearest medium and attend a seance, remember that the means to communicate with the spirit world…MAY BE ONLY A TELEPHONE CALL AWAY!

Questions Pertaining to the Subject of the Immortality of the Soul

There are literally hundreds—if not thousands—of questions we could ask about the world hereafter. Many wish to know about the location of the world of spirits, the appearance of those who dwell in other dimensions, as well as the customs that prevail in these heavenly societies. We're interested in knowing if we are permitted to eat in the great beyond, will we find our relatives waiting for us, will we have a love life, will we be entertained, or are we destined to float around on a cloud for all eternity playing the harp dressed only in a white gown?

A person could literally spend eternity—at least in our time frame—theorizing about such matters, and then who knows just how right we might or might not be.

Naturally, both Tim and I have pondered these very matters, discussing them endlessly upon getting together for periodic brain storming sessions.

One of the most frequently asked questions is do souls eat, sleep, make love, or simply lounge around in the great beyond?

The answer to these cannot be given in absolute words which will be applicable to everyone. If you make love with your eternal bondmate, for example, it is indeed a beautiful, eternal and cosmically rewarding experience. Love exists in heavenly dimensions as it does here. However, in the higher planes, love is more closely associated with a blending of spirits so that two become literally as one. I doubt very much if you'll find single's bars, and one night stands just do not exist as they would be of benefit to neither party. On the higher planes—as we become atuned with God's true vibrations—love becomes more universal in nature, and we find that our spirits no longer crave the comfort of another soul to offer comfort and support. Until we have obtained these heights, however, we do strike up lasting relationships with other spirits who are on our same wave length.

As for eating, well, some souls have progressed only to the stage in their earthly life where they need "fancy food," in order to maintain mental and physical balance. Some souls of goodness who are definitely headed for heavenly dimensions still will enjoy the pleasures of eating, though it will be done solely for taste sensations since consuming food is not necessary to stay "alive" in these other realms. Eventually, all of us will progress beyond this point, though it could take us quite some time, depending upon how much we learn after crossing over.

Meeting Love Ones

Now comes the matter of meeting up with loved ones, friends and relatives in the afterlife. The truth is—and be prepared for a possible shock—if you disliked your parents while you were on earth and never got along, you will not have to suffer meeting up with them in heaven. If your marriage was a bad one (say your wife tried to poison you), there is no need to suffer and prolong the pain after you've "gone." If a relationship was not generally blissful and you have no desire to confront that individual ever again, your soul will not meet up with theirs. What would be the purpose?

During a lifetime, certain souls form links with other souls. Usually this happens easily and naturally within the family structure; the most obvious example is the mother/child link. Just as the mother and child blend life-blood during the time that the baby is in the womb, so it is that the life-force, the spirits of both mother and child, blend during a lifetime.

Once in a while, the mother-child relationship is not that good and one or both do not wish to be psychically/spiritually linked to the other for lifetime after lifetime. In this case, it is the right of the soul not to blend with the other. Occasionally there is a "karmic debt" which keeps two souls together, lifetime after lifetime, for better or for worse. This type of life-after-life link can be examined and explained by a gifted psychic if the person involved wants this understanding, which stretches passed one lifetime.

If a link is not made within the family, often two very good friends, lovers, or marriage partners form a spiritual link. In this case, these precious and infinite friends await on the other side.

The bottom line is, if the two soul-forces are tied together, they will find each other again after "death" for they have formed a bond which is larger than both of them and which survives death in the mundane dimension. Theirs is a consciousness which is tuned into the same "cosmic station, and so they will naturally meet on the other side.

It is traditional universal law that the bond-partner who made the transition first guides the newly-transitioned partner through the period of death of the physical body and shines alight into the heaven-world of the beyond.

Seldom is there a problem with, for instance, one's mother being on one level of heaven, guiding one onward during the transition and one's marriage partner, with whom a cosmic bond has been formed, awaiting on another level of heaven. Usually the person making the transition to the afterworld has formed a more definite link with one level of consciousness or the other. However, if there is conflict, gentle guidance from the Higher Realms will make the decision an apparent and easy one as the transition is made. It truly depends on what level the person making the transition is on; if you would not be comfortable at an extremely high level of consciousness, for instance, you will seek your own level slightly less exalted but still within heaven. Perhaps your mother had reached an extremely high level of consciousness whereas you and your marriage/bondmate (soulmate) had reached a level with which you both felt comfortable...which was home. In that case, you will go home. Home is your level of consciousness, your frequency, your vibration. It is the drummer to which your spirit marches. It is where you truly feel at ease. It is *your* dimension!

Martin Luther King Speaks

Many important and influential world leaders, scientists, religious figures and the famous in general who have passed on, still try to guide our actions in order to make the earth a better reality in which to live. Churchill, for instance, comes across the dimensional barrier frequently to give us discourses, as does the likes of Washington, Lincoln, and Kennedy. If you're more into a "pop" oriented lifestyle no need to fret as Elvis Presley and John Lennon also give forth with pearls of wisdom from their new homes.

Since his assassination, black leader Dr. Martin Luther King has spoken through a very unlikely medium. Florence Gunn at age sixty was entirely skeptical about psychical matters, not being at all informed on parapsychology or spiritual science. Nevertheless, her life became changed when voices started popping into her head. These voices purported to be from departed souls. Ms. Gunn began keeping a record of the messages she received. On Good Friday she heard for the first time from Dr. King who continues to want to see the world we reside on become a better place in which to live.

And how does Martin Luther King see heaven?

"I behold the glory of the Lord. I am with Him now. All is well with me but is it well with my people? Who will care for them now? There is much to be done for them...I am happy here because I am useful. Could anyone be useful or happy if just walking golden streets, wearing a white robe and singing all day long? What a useless life that would be! No one, but no one, would enjoy it for more than a little while. We need work into which we can put our spiritual hearts..No, we do not hurry and get out of breath here. Neither do we walk the golden streets or loll around in luxurious idleness. We are orderly, busy, neither hurried nor flurried."

Are spirits then expected to be perfect? According to Dr. King this concept isn't necessarily true. "We make mistakes here just as we did on earth. Being here does not mean that we suddenly become perfect, but we can see further, deeper than we did on earth..."

The Disembodiment of Man

Neither Tim or I profess to know all there is to know about the afterlife, such a study would take several decades. But one man, Dr. Paschal Beverly Randolph, M.D., put 50 years of his life into such an avocation. Reading all the available literature (religious, historical and psychic texts), as well as interviewing those who had near death experiences, or who claimed to have communicated with spirits, is how the good doctor formulated his opinions.

Many, many years go, Dr. Randolph put together a 200,000 word manuscript titled *After Death—The Disembodiment of Man* which was based upon his seasoned research. The topics he covered are vast and utterly boundless—just as the regions of heaven are. In order to wet your appetite for more knowledge on this subject, we have drawn from this very literate work to give the reader a better idea of what it's like in the next world. We have broken Dr. Randolph's thinking down into various categories to make for easier reading.

Spiritual Beings of Other Worlds—Size and Shape

The size of an ethereal person is, but not invariably, such as, were they solid substance, would balance from eighty to one hundred and fifteen pounds; albeit, there are in some of the spiritual zones very tiny people indeed, who, having been occasionally seen by earth-dwellers, have been christened Fairies, Fays, and Banshees. There are others ten feet and over in height; while on the farther zones there are people wholly and totally dissimilar in all respects from those of this solar system. Here is the law: Large earths produce large creatures; small earths, small; and if our moon's inhabitants ever reach the human plane, they will not exceed the height of thirty inches; while the people of Jupiter, Herschel, and Saturn, are a great deal larger and finer than ourselves. The size of the planet also determines the law of duration. We are old men when Jupiterians are mere boys; and their school children would laugh at the mental imbecility of our profoundest savants.

An ethereal man cannot penetrate solid matter while organized. Were he enclosed in an iron coffin he would pass through its pores as sweat through the cuticle, re-form on the outside, and consider it a very unpleasant experiment, not to be repeated. An ethereal man could not be annihilated by any means whatever, even though blown from a thousand cannons. Such a thing would shock a man, and incapacitate him from thinking clearly for a time, but that is all.

Retaining Physical Characteristics

Do we retain our physical characteristics, as hair, eyes, and so forth, in the other life?

To a certain extent, as to general form of features, save that deformities are toned down. Our red and other colored hair here, is of a general flaxen hue there; it is long and flowing; we are beardless, except as we choose to assume the contrary appearance. Fat men lose their fatness. Nearly all of us there are of a beautiful olive-pearly tint, with the peach-rose in either cheek; our eyes are both light and dark, but not violently so; the tall man becomes shorter; the stumpy man or dwarf increases in stature; and the lank skeleton attains to beautiful and harmonious proportions.

Language, Beauty, Growing Up

In reference to vocal language, it is used. At first we speak in our native tongues; but rapidly learn others, because hearing the sounds that convey a man's meaning, and at the same time both feeling and seeing his thought, we soon acquire what otherwise would necessitate long study. The tendency of all vocal speech there is towards a universal Phonetic system, and in the upper grades such is universally used. But there also we have two other modes of conveying information: one of which is the reading of thoughts, the other, by conforming our features to the required expression, which is readily understood by the developed initiates.

Dr. Randolph formulated the following idea. 1st. That children grow up there as here; and 2nd, that females *generally,* though not universally, appear as matrons of from thirty-five to fifty years. Men generally appear of from thirty to forty-five; while occasionally one is seen *a la* patriarch, and many as mere lads. A few of earth's celebrities are famous there; not because they were kings and generals, but by reason of the parts played in the moral, political, and religious worlds. Thus, Buddha, Pythagoras, Luther, Plato, and others, are the centers of great attention and attraction still.

The standards of beauty vary there, according to the tastes of different constitutions, nations, and customs. Purity and intellect generally are the criteria; for, as these are possessed, they are reflected on the countenance.

Books and Kings

It is asked if there are books there; and I reply yes; but not such as we have. They are on scrolls, not pages, and are picture-written, not type-written or morocco-bound. There are libraries to which all who wish have access.

Are there kings and rulers there? Yes. But these, except in the lower regions, are such by natural, spontaneous gravitation and selection. Mistakes are never made, for the reason that the right man glides into the right place by a natural process.

Are nations distinct there? At first, and on the lesser planes, yes; but soon a great intercommingling takes place, as individuals rise from, and gravitate out of conditions tending to isolation and non-progress. Whoever would ascertain the condition of the dead of a million years ago must quit the boundaries of this solar system, for none from it are in that sphere, and search for them among the constellar zones of space, where they exist in myriads.

Occupations and Relationships

The next question on the list concerns our occupations in the worlds of ethereal people. To fully reply to it would require not one, but an entire library of books.

(a) We retain and acknowledge no relationship there, save such as we have love and friendship for a basis. My father is not necessarily related to me, *merely* because he was the channel through which I came to earth; nor is my mother any nearer to me simply because she received the monad Me, incarnated it in a flesh- and-blood body; nursed me for seven years, more or less, and called me her son and darling. Ties, blood, race, or family, count for little or nothing over there; for it continually happens, as said before, that the veriest stranger is nearer and dearer than husband, wife, parent, sister, child, or brother; say, even than those we sometimes believe to be our "Eternal Affinities." And one of our occupations there is the study of the laws that govern this subject.

Kindred there is based on homeogeneity, not on consanguinity or external law. We love those who love what we do, and these are our brethren and sisters. Two cannon-balls are not necessarily related because cast in the same mould; nor are people brothers or sisters merely because their parents were the same; for their natures may be, and often are, wholly opposite and antagonistic. Nor is it unusual to see a coarse, rough, brutal, lowly-organized man, and a 'girl born of the same couple, who is fine, gentle, sensitive, intellectual, and spiritual, to a very high degree. Where's the relationship? In what does it consist? The study, then, of psychical law, will afford scope for the best minds in the spiritual worlds.

Names

(b) "What's in a name?" some one asks. A great deal, I reply. There are long catalogues of names, and what they represent, to be learned, and in one single branch of nomenclature, that of botany, we have abundant occupation in the study. Then there is architecture, history, algebra, the higher mathematics, government, ideology, phonetics, music, melody, harmony, vision, acoustics, and ten thousand other arts and sciences to engage our attention and occupy our thoughts. Speaking of names, reminds me that those given us or assumed here, go for naught in our upper homes. There are no John Smiths there; nor is Mynheer Johannes Von der Spreuchtlinsaber any longer compelled to respond, when hailed by that formidable appellation. We convey information to other souls telepathically for the most part, so they know by our vibrations when we are directing our thoughts to them.

(c) Old names, then, are dropped, soon after our arrival there —albeit, if an earthly sufferer yearns for the ministrations of an ethereal friend, whose name might once have been John Truman, or William Hardy, his electric summons will reach him in the upper land, wherever he may be. Every person's quality is expressed upon the features, just as the unspoken thought is mirrored on the tablet of consciousness. Like that, too, it can be read, unless, indeed, as is possible in both cases,—but only by a painful, continued effort—the person wills to conceal the thought, or give a false impression to the features—and that general quality, or a peculiar trait determines the name by which the person will be known. Now, the combination of qualities and traits are simply infinite, and so are the names of the myriads who possess them. No two are alike. No language could express this multitude of qualities and specialties.

That can only be achieved through and by the celestial phonetics of the spheres. For instance, Olive Selk, of Janesville, Honey Lake Valley, California, was the peerless and redeeming spirit of that town,—a gentle, tender, affectionate, and loving soul,—qualities expressed in the higher phonetics by the sounds ZOI-LI-VI—IA; hence her most beautiful name will be ZOLIVIA. Mary Winthrop may on earth possess qualities, social and intellectual, which not only stamped her as a genius, but also made her the cherished idol of society. She will therefore be known as EU-LAM-PI-IA,—*Eulampia,* Greek, *Evlambea,* Anglice, *Bright-Shining Light.*

The Senses

Roses emit sweet odors, yet not all the fragrance of the Gulistan, ten thousand times refined, can equal the blessed aromas that float upon the breezes of the happy land of educated souls! Color: Prismatic hues are fine; the flash of sparkling diamonds transcendently beautiful, while the play of colors in polarized light is vastly more splendid still; but no man of earth, save through clairvoyant intromission,—and that is extremely rare,— ever yet saw, or even imagined, the superlatively magnificent melody of hues and tints, or the ineffable brilliance and glorious beauty of the flowers blooming there!

Music

Ah, how shall cold human language convey an idea or sense of the transcendent melodies, tones, and exquisite sounds heard and *felt* in the upper divisions of the spirits' home, whereof I am writing? It is impossible! I dare not undertake the hopeless task; and yet it will, one day, be described. Those who have listened to *Offenbach's* opera, *La Duchess de Gerolstein,* will remember the exquisite orchestral overture to the third act, just before Fritz's disaster. Well, I am *positively* certain that that piece of music came to him complete, and note by note, from the Spirit Land!

Scenery

Imagine your-highest ideal spread out before you; deck it with the most regal and imperial cities, every house of which shall be a perfect palace; surround it with parks, adorned with trees, whose fruit and foliage shall be unequalled save in a poet's or a lover's dream; let there roam beneath these trees, or stand under their outspread branches, parties and groups of loving men and women, all of whose forms are fair and faultless; females of transcendent grace and beauty; men looking every inch as kings, of intellect, and royal, gentle manhood; children lovely as the summer sunshine, gay as mountain-birds; animals, compared to whose forms that of the gazelle is dull, tame, and crooked; and when you have all this in your mind's eye, believe me when I say, it is no more equal to the reality up there than a cedar swamp is to a king's garden!

Taste

Flavors! wait till the nectar is quaffed and the ambrosia tasted by yourself—for no human tongue can tell, no pen explain them, or even intimate their scale or gamut.

Touch

Contact! Ah, my God! I have attempted, and may again, attempt to describe them; but as I look at my descriptions, glowing and impassioned though they be, I am sensible of having failed to convey even a dim and faint notion of the thrilling raptures and exquisite joys of touch and contact awaiting us all over there, and now being experienced by countless billions who have gone before!

Peace, Feasts and Plenty

Buddha's Loaks, the Moslem's Paradise, and The Christian's Heaven are conceptions cold and tame, compared with the realities of man's home in the higher divisions.

There blessed peace reigns supreme; harmonious melody prevails; God, not man, or creeds, or a book, is there devoutly worshiped; love underlies, will compels, and lofty wisdom directs all movement there. Rest and labor alternate, God rules through magic-working law, to which all most joyfully assent; order prevails on every hand, and chaos is unknown!

Feasts, parties, balls, operas, concerts, the drama, straws, schools, colleges, universities, libraries, museums, lectures, theatres, orations, celebrations, congresses, elections, coronations—in fact everything good that man here enjoys, he also has there, in the upper country, with the exception of genuine law courts, churches, baptisms, and funerals; and some of the glorious scenes there exhibited immeasurably surpass the most ecstatic vision of poet, voluptuary, enthusiast, or dreamer.

Education

The scope, sweep, and extent of the entire human being must ever enlarge: mental, like physical motion, gives heat, and heat expands its subject and object. As we advance in the spirit, as in this life, new, higher, and better and nobler ideals are conceived, and we are impelled by the law within to work up to, and act on, those ideals, whatever they may be; and whether they interest the personal, social, moral, aesthetic, religious, or intellectual departments of our nature. New possibilities will ever be attempted and achieved, albeit nothing whatever can permanently fill the pressure will expand them and thus make room for more ere tomorrow shall end. True, the soul may rest satisfied for a while, and a long while; but the monotony will at last be broken, and it will sight and seek for change. Action is the law of true life, multiplied and varied action. Eternal sameness means eternal stagnation.

Never Alone

The love of thirty years is not the love of eighteen or forty-five. No one goes alone from earth to Spirit Land. Some loving one is always by his side or hers, from the last breath till eternity grows bald and grey. No one goes alone from one grand division to another; no one can gravitate from a low to a higher state before he or she is fully fit to do so, and then they graduate in couples. But it does not follow that those loving classmates or kindly ones are ever the same persons. It were a poor heaven if only one true soul sincerely loved us. If comrade A, in division three, is not prepared to go with B to division four, then A's place is immediately taken by C or D, who are prepared, and the union thus based on *fitness,* for far closer than that just dissolved.

No Two Souls Alike

"As like as two peas!" Well, no two peas are alike, nor any two persons in existence; no two souls can develop alike, in all respects and at the same rate, because no two can be exactly similar; and if they were, the chances are a million to one that this one forges a little ahead of the other, or that one springs a mine without the other's sphere. The chances are infinitely against their remaining alike for any given period. Their earthly experiences could not have been parallel, and a single reminiscence, a memory, may beget a change that will establish a divergence of eternal duration. A tone heard, a flash of light, motion seen or felt by one of the parties, may beget a movement that in time would completely change the entire mental and emotional constitution, just as continued grains of poison would modify the body that took them. For this reason, then, that no two souls can forever develop in parallel lines, one of them must, in time, diverge from, advance beyond, rise above, or constitutionally change, outgrow or off grow the other; the "eternal" affinity must be considerably foreshortened and lopped off here and there, until common sense makes all clear, plain, right, and the Infinite wisdom be vindicated. Yet souls are made in pairs; but this involves perpetual *friendship,* but by no means eternal marriage, it requires *opposites* for that; but our twin is very like ourself.

Education

In this fifth division there are many colleges and universities, in which spirit, its laws, static and dynamic, are taught. Memory, the laws of thought; the statics of life; the principles of social evolution; light, its sources and nature; esoteric laws of life; embryology; the integral and differential calculus, direct and in their application to various branches of human learning; philosophy, astronomy, paralactic calculations; the higher mathematics, algebra, and the true theory of the higher equations, psychological law, and a hundred sciences not yet evolved by, or sent down to, man on earth; the laws and dynamics of beauty, harmony, melody, form, government, religion, God, the laws governing friendship, affection, love, the source of the generation and growth of thought, and a thousand things beside.

The people are extremely refined, and seem to have decreased in size from what they were in the grade below. They partake of fruits and various aromas, bathe for pleasure's sake and certain ends to be obtained, and already explained. They are mainly sustained by what they absorb and inhale. They sleep, as do all others, and are refreshed thereby. There are no crowded cities; nor is the scene entirely rural; but their houses, cots, and palaces are scattered at convenient distances apart over a vast area of surface. They frequently visit the divisions above and below them, and occasionally they visit other realms of human abode, just as we here are intromitted to higher ranges of being occasionally.

Eternal Youth

Reader, come with me and share this vision; gaze upon these glories—all to be yours—and mine—one of these approaching years. Look down yonder sylvan glade, and behold these hundreds upon hundreds of sylph-like human beings of either sex. They are not of our times, or our form of mind; they are Phoenicians, Babylonians, Ninevites, Arabs, Persians, Egyptians, Hindoos, Moors, Chinese, and some from Central Africa, some from Greece, and some from old Etruria, and the site of storied Troy. Many of them immigrated from earth ten thousand years ago—some longer than that; and very few of them less than half that vast period over five and thirty years of age! They have drunk at the fountain of perpetual youth and partaken of the fruit of the life-conferring tree. The females! How like peerless queens of Grace and Beauty! What holy love and tenderness beam from every eye! What melting passion dwells on every lip! How like clouds of lovely glory they move along; and what amazing perfection sits crowned on every feature! And all of them were once poor, weak mortals like you and I; vexed at a trifle, pleased at a straw; small in spirit, cramped in mind, and warped in soul, heedless of all but what the fleeting hour afforded of pain-mixed joy!

● ● ●

But, regardless of what Dr. Randolph's thinking may be we must always remember that the only instrument we have to perceive our reality (our dimension) at this very moment is our mind/soul. It is exactly the same in the heavenly dimensions!

God and the heavenly hosts always "stand at the door and knock." They are one with us through our intuitive gifts (truly divine conduits to God) and through the goodness of our heart and soul. It is the easiest thing in the world to be in contact with God and with the heavenly hosts. What is not so easy is to know absolutely, beyond a shadow of a doubt, that God lives within us, within our souls…as well as on the outside, in the universe. Your soul *is* the God-spark! It is assured a place in the heavenly dimension of its choice if only it *knows* this, instinctively and intuitively. This is true awareness…the awareness of one's rightful place within the cosmic scheme of it all. You are important even though you are a mere particular in the vastness of God's universe. You are made of "cosmic stuff," you are made of "holy stuff." The very life-force which gives you energy to take a breath and to keep your body's heart beating proves beyond a shadow of a doubt that you are "magical" (your soul is "magical.!). You are eternal for you *are* mind-energy and mind-energy cannot be destroyed. God gave you this mind-energy which is so magical and so mystical. God gave you a particle of Himself/Herself when He gave you LIFE. Rest assured that this lifespark will move onward to its rightful heavenly home!

UFOs—How Do They Tie In With the Dead

As veteran researchers of the UFO phenomena, we have come across some very bizarre stories in our line of work. And while the public may have no way of being aware of the actual intricacies of this worldwide enigma, those who have plotted and probed the appearance of so-called flying saucers, can tell you that not all UFOs are nuts and bolts hardware from space, but some seem to be a type of ethereal apparition.

Rev. Billy Graham has suggested in his writings that a percentage of UFOs might actually be angels. After all, religious texts often describe how these heavenly beings arrive in a brilliance that is so stunning to the eye as to make a person go momentarily blind. Also, in the majority of cases, the crews of these glittering vessels appear to be humanoid in appearance, though perhaps just a bit too beautiful to be earthly in origin. Biblical students will confirm that the angels of the Old Testament were said to be so exactly like us that they would often come into a person's house and eat a meal with them. The only way that someone could tell they were not "ordinary" was by the fact that they sometimes had a strange halo or glow about them, and besides they are always said to be extremely beautiful. A mere coincidence? We'll let you decide.

Now, here's an absolutely fascinating episode that came to our attention five or six years ago. A woman was driving along an isolated stretch of road in Indiana when she saw this circular-shaped device come down and block the path of her automobile so that she could not continue on her way home. Though she was frightened the woman could not move. It was as if she were paralyzed. Shortly, a hatchway on the side of the craft opened and two beings came out walking directly toward where she was seated, frozen behind the steering wheel of her car.

"One of the men stood in the shadows and I could not see him plainly at first," Norma told her tale, a trace of bewilderment obvious in the tone of her voice. "This one fellow, however, came to within a foot or so of my half opened window. He did not speak, but still I could hear him talking to me if that makes any sense. He said that he meant me no harm, and he wanted to know if my name was Norma. Well, to say the least, I was totally shocked, that this complete stranger—and I mean that in its truest sense—would know who I was, especially since I was certain he wasn't even from the same world I lived on. Somehow, I managed to choke out an answer and to inquire as to what he wanted with me. In my mind flashed the following words, 'We've come to show you that you are immortal, that life goes on even after death.'"

At that the second figure who had been off to the side stepped out of the darkness and Norma found herself in total shock.

"The man who approached me was dressed in coveralls of some type, and his head was slightly elongated, though otherwise, he could easily pass as one of us. But the second fellow, well, I'd know him anywhere. He was dressed in an ordinary shirt and a pair of jeans. The second figure was that of my deceased husband who had been killed in a hunting accident about seven or eight months back."

Norma couldn't control herself. "I began to weep uncontrollably and with my tears came the thought, 'Fear not my darling, as I am with you always in the clouds!' The voice was unmistakably that of my beloved husband who as far as I was concerned had passed away almost a year ago."

Was there a possibility that she might have been in error, that her encounter with a UFO might have caused her severe mental trauma and that she was imagining at least this part of the experience?

"Absolutely not!. Norma insists. "I'd know my George anywhere."

And how did he look?

"Better than he had at the prime of his life," comes the widow's response. "He looked slightly ill and pale toward the end, but now he was standing straight, had lost ten-or fifteen pounds, and the color had come back to his face."

With this, the beings reentered the device that still rested on the roadway, and within seconds it had vanished, traveling at incredible speed straight up into the star filled heavens.

The Case for George Adamski's Return

A peculiar story we'd agree, but this incident does not by any means stand alone in the history of UFOlogy.

Take the case investigated by British flying saucer investigator, Jimmy Goddard who attended a lecture on June 7, 1965 and found himself in the middle of a most bizarre tale.

"A most unusual incident began on June 7th at about 10:30 p.m. and the witness, an M. Bryant, was just going to bed at his home in Scorriton (England) when he heard a sound like that of a ship's turbine. He looked outside and saw a pale blue light travelling west to east at an altitude of 300 to 400 feet. He saw this come down, then the light and the noise disappeared.

"Next day he looked over the area and found strange pieces of metal, some like turbines with curved blades, and some looking like more complicated pieces of machinery. Also there was a glass phial with some silver sand in it (later analyzed and found with certainty to be silver sand), also in the phial was a message 'adelphos adelpho' (brother to brother) in what appeared to be classical Greek. There was also an evil-smelling patch of jelly-like substance where the object had appeared to land, but this quickly evaporated.

"Late that same year (1965) Mr. Oliver, in his capacity as membership secretary of BUFORA, sent a questionnaire round to as many interested people as possible, and one of the questions was: 'Have you ever had a sighting or contact?' One of these forms was sent to Mr. Bryant describing an—extraordinary contact claim in which the witness claimed, on April 24th, 1965, to have met with beings from outer space, spoken with them and entered their saucer.

"On the day in question he was going for a walk from his home to Scorriton Down, and when he arrived there he turned to look back toward the village. He saw a large saucer appear out of thin air over the field, then descend to about three feet altitude and hover there. An opening appeared in the middle of the saucer, and a door appeared to slide upward. Three beings, all dressed in 'diving gear' (complete with helmets) came out, and one of them beckoned wildly to Mr. Bryant."

Goddard continues in his communication to this writer by saying that Bryant went over to them, and as he did so they took off their helmets. "Two of them were definitely not of this world—they had very long foreheads, blue eyes, (which reminded Mr. Bryant of cats' eyes,, blond hair and squat noses. Their mouths appeared bluish, but Mr. Oliver said that this could be a reaction to our atmosphere. The suits were one-piece and silvery in color, and when the beings moved the sound suggested tinfoil. They had belts with a strange 'sun' or 'flower petal' symbol on them.

"The helmets had windows in them which appeared to be of a per-spex-like substance, and at a place corresponding with the ears there were strange coils.

"The third occupant was different from the other two, although dressed in a similar suit. He had the appearance of a 14 year old boy with black hair, and the suit appeared to be too big for him. He had what Mr. Bryant described as a 'mid-European accent with a touch of American.'"

Goddard then says that this third being talked to Mr. Bryant and this is the gist of what he said: "One month from today we will bring proof of Mantell. Watch for the blue light in the evening. Danger of forces from Epsilon who take people from procreation purposes. These cause what you call poltergeist which are only invisible because of your ignorance of the orbital plane. My name is Yamski."

When asked where he was from he said, "From Venus. If only Des or Les were here, he would understand." Mr. Bryant then asked if he could arrange, for "Des or Les" to see him, and Yamski replied, "No, we will arrange for them to see you."

Goddard continues with his communication by stating that after this "Mr. Bryant was helped up into the ship (still hovering at about 3 feet) and found inside that it was made of several identical compartments. In each one there was a door leading in the floor like the one through which he had entered.. There was a couch in each compartment, fitted with straps, and a large screen similar to a TV screen on which rainbow-colored lights appeared to be moving upward. Mr. Bryant asked how the craft was propelled, and he was told, 'Ideo motor movement.'

"Shortly after this he was taken out of the craft, which then ascended to about 40 feet, then vanished in the same manner in which it had arrived."

Unless you have a background in UFO research, or have read a ton of books on the subject, chances are you will immediately want to dismiss the entire episode as hogwash before even making a stab at going any further. But just let us get a word in edgewise and say that in the last three—close to four—decades since UFOs have become a worldwide phenomena, over two thousand individuals spread across the planet have reportedly come in contact with some type of alien being. Often these stories seem totally off the wall and one's first honest reaction would be to say that the witness was a bit daffy, but incredibly enough often those involved are highly thought of, very sincere individuals, who seem to have no motive for lying, nor have they had a history of mental disorder or hallucinating.

Something strange is definitely going on in the heavens directly above us...but the question remains, what does all this mean?

Mr. Oliver, Britain's top authority on UFOs we're convinced had no prior knowledge about interplanetary craft, but yet, he appeared to be telling his experience in all earnest as if it had actually happened.

Even more remarkable was the fact that Mr. Oliver had absolutely no way of knowing that an individual by the name of George *Adamski* (sounding nearly the same as *Yamski*) had died a scant two days earlier in a Washington, D.C. hospital. Adamski, for those who are not familiar with this name, was one of the earliest of UFO contactees. As far back as October, 1946, this mild mannered man of Polish descent, had been among thousands of San Diego residents who were startled to see a gigantic spaceship hovering over a nearby mountain range. The craft returned over a period of several years and it was from these observations that Adamski was curious about who piloted these silvery craft and was confident that he could make contact with their occupants.

In November, 1952, Adamski heard that some of these ships had actually been seen coming down in the California desert. So on November 20, 1952, Adamski invited a group of friends to accompany him to the desert for a picnic and to look for saucers. Parking off the main highway, it was only a half hour before their "saucer-watch" drew positive results. Attracted first by the sounds of a plane's motors, they "suddenly and simultaneously," saw close to the nearest mountain range a "gigantic cigar-shaped silvery shin, without wings or appendages of any kind." The craft seemed to drift in their direction, then stopped and hovered motionless.

Adamski excitedly told those with him to remain where they were while he approached the object at a closer range.

Setting up his camera equipment, Adamski saw a scout ship maneuver between nearby mountain peaks. The craft proceeded to land and a being got out. He was about 5 feet 6 inches in height and looked to be about 150 pounds. Adamski described him as having "an extremely high forehead; large, but calm, gray-green eyes, slightly aslant at the outer corners; with slightly higher cheek bones than an Occidental, but not as high as an Indian or an Oriental; a finely chiselled nose, not conspicuously large; and an average size mouth with beautiful white teeth.

Through the use of sign language and telepathy, Adamski was able to find out that this being-came from the planet Venus. Although he had landed in the desert in a small scout ship, he indicated that all travel outside the atmosphere of Earth was done in a larger carrier or "mother ship." After a few more minutes, and a few more questions on Adamski's part, the space visitor climbed back into his parked ship and took off. Adamski then returned to the waiting party who later signed affidavits to the effect that such an encounter had actually transpired.

The rest of Adamski's story is history. Before passing from this dimension he wrote several books detailing his encounters with fair-haired space beings (*Flying Saucers Have Landed, Inside the Space Ships* and Flying *Saucers Farewell*). His first effort was co-authored by a British historian whose name was—are you ready—DESMOND LESLIE.

Yamski had proclaimed during his meeting with Mr. Bryant that if only "Des" or "Les" were present, that he would know what was going on.

Coincidence? Imagination? A visual hallucination? A damn pack of lies?

All the above could be the explanation to this case history, but maybe—JUST MAYBE!—Mr. Bryant was on the level. In his favor was the fact that investigators saw no traces of UFO literature in the witness' home, nor did he have a history of being interested in the occult or supernatural. Instead, the interviewers found Mr. Bryant to be about 50 years old, married with three children. He told them further that the saucer had the appearance of platinum, and that the sheep in a nearby field had seemed unconcerned during the time the ship hovered, but when it left they turned their heads as if to follow the flight of the craft which he could not see.

Yamski also mentioned the name Mantell...well Captain Thomas Mantell was the name of a U.S. Air Force pilot who was killed over the state of Kentucky when his fighter plane got too close to a gigantic disc-shaped object, and he lost oxygen and plunged to the ground where he was killed instantly.

The Case of Uncle Roy

Now let's take a case from Diane Tessman's files and do our best to compare it to the above episode just before we try to make heads or tails out of the situation of how UFOs tie in with the dead.

There are several cases I know of where a person has died in the regular world and has then been spotted in a UFO encounter. One in particular has to do with a man we shall call "Uncle Roy"—who had pursued his interests in UFOs, metaphysics, and heavenly dimensions throughout his life. Some of his relatives even made fun of this interest. Uncle Roy was not married but his nephew James lived with him on his small farm in Indiana, helping him care for a small herd of cows, chickens, and helping tend the fields. I interviewed James shortly after Uncle Roy's death and the young man had turned from a pessimist who gently had made fun of Uncle Roy's beliefs to a true believer in the paranormal and UFOs in particular. He gives the following account: "Uncle Roy always claimed he'd been visited by these UFO beings back in his early manhood when he was out there on the back field, getting it ready for the spring planting...but I never really believed him. Oh, I thought that he thought he was telling the truth but I just sort of figured that Uncle Roy was unique and that sometimes he told tall stories that even he believed." James shakes his head and lights a cigarette. "That's what I *used to* believe. Now I betcha I sound just like Uncle Roy to you. I bet you are thinking that I believe this story, but that I'm just a crazy farm boy."

I assured James that I myself have had UFO encounters and experiences and that I found his account fascinating and not hard to believe at all.

James continued, "Uncle Roy died in the same back field, you know. He had a sudden massive heart attack and was dead when I found him several minutes later. We had him buried right and proper and that should have been the end of it, according to most people. But two days later, I was just coming out the front door, here, when I saw a bright, glowing light shining over the house...oh, about 50 feet right out from where we are standing right now. It was just getting to be sunset and at first I told myself it was the sun. However, it landed right out there, where the front field meets the back field as it sort of winds around there. It landed, I tell you! And I swear to you that it was a small, saucer shaped craft...not like anything our military has at all.

"It just came straight down and sat there for a while, still sort of glowing but not as much. It has a goldish-orange color to the glow. I didn't move off the porch...but finally I did go down the steps and got to within about 40 feet. The hatch door opened and, I swear to you on my mother's grave...Uncle Roy stepped into the light from within the ship, at the very top of the hatch door...and waved to me. He didn't get out, mind you...he just waved once, real friendly like. I got the feeling in my heart that he was saying he was happy now. He was finally with his friends..."

103

James stopped talking for a moment, hesitated, and then went on.

"These were the friends he kept telling me about who he met in the field in his younger days. You know, I saw them too...and now I wait for them—just like Uncle Roy did!"

This case is but a single example of several the authors know of in which persons who have died have later been seen aboard a UFO, happily at home with the crew and traveling presumably among the stars.

We must be careful here, however, and not jump to any hasty conclusions. We can't assume for a moment that all UFO occupants previously lived on earth and are now freely roaming the heavens in the afterlife.

From our study of metaphysics, what seems to be happening is that upon his passing Uncle Roy's soul passed from our dimension frequency into a heavenly frequency which he chose before his passing, though he might not have been conscious of what he was doing. His constant dwelling on UFOs and the friendly space folk he met drew his soul to their dimension since they were operating on the same frequency. It would be apparent to our thinking at least, that if you believe strongly enough in extraterrestrial beings and feel that you are one with them, that when your time comes to "cross over" from this plane to another, you might wind up where you feel the most at home.

Remember, the authors have studied UFOs for many years (having had personal experiences ourselves—enough to fill several books), and we realize fully well that a good percentage of the beings who are onboard these craft are much more spiritually evolved than we earthlings are. The space brothers, as we lovingly call them, have learned to lift their consciousness and their vibrations so that they have become ethereal and not physical in composition.

A good friend of ours whom we mentioned previously, Gabriel Green of Yucca Valley, California, is very happy today even though his charming, much beloved wife, is no longer with him in a physical sense. Gabe knows that she is able to communicate with him from her rather lofty position aboard a large mothership that hangs invisible over the California desert sending down loving vibrations in an attempt to lift the consciousness of the population of the west coast.

As we shall see in the following chapter, the space people have a definite purpose in making themselves known at this time. Their appearance has to do with the physical death of the Planet; a world that is much like we humans who inhabit it...in that it has a spirit and a soul which will continue to live on, even if the world itself should be destroyed.

Will Earth Merge with the Heavens in the New Age?

Great physical, mental and spiritual changes are taking place on earth and will continue to do so as we progress toward the end of this century. These changes—some of which will be disastrous—will effect each and everyone of us, both positively and negatively. The earth will rumble with earthquakes and volcanic activity, the weather will shift drastically, entire continents will rise, while others will sink into the sea in the twinkling of an eye.

Every psychic, every UFO contactee and every spiritual leader from Billy Graham on, see "great changes" in the months and years just ahead. And now, even those reporting near death experiences are now coming forward to tell of their being able to peer into the future and witness the upheaval that is to strike.

What all these same "awakened" individuals also report observing from their lofty perch out of the physical body, is a new age, or golden age which will come immediately after this period of strife.

Dr. Kenneth Ring, mentioned earlier in this volume for his research into afterlife phenomenon, has recently updated his findings in a book titled *Heading toward Omega*. In his new work published by William Morrow, Dr. Ring, once again interviewed patients who had "died" and come back to life. Many of those he spoke with trembled as they told him of a future in which humankind would live in peace and would prosper, and mankind would be one with nature and with God. Dr. Ring's patients spoke of harmony and universal brotherhood, and a spiritual awakening like none that has gone before.

My own contacts with interdimensional beings would lead me to believe that while there is great turmoil ahead for us, eventually the wicked will perish through their own deeds, and those of goodness and light will progress to unheralded heights and will go on to live in a truly "Golden Age" of abundance, good health, enhanced psychic powers and a knowledge of God's role in their everyday lives. During this period of turmoil, many whose vibrations remain pure will be lifted from this planet in spaceships and will be housed in great motherships or satellite cities which are now in orbit around our planet, but which remain invisible as they exist in higher realms as of the present time.

Evidently, the late 1900s hold something special for the human race. Some feel that this is a wonderful time in which the heavenly dimensions and our physical state of being will merge and start to work in unison. At that point many of us will possess enhanced powers of extrasensory perception and will be able to travel from dimension to dimension without difficulty in craft which we will be able to power with our minds. This is the same period when Jesus will return and we along with the Son of God will be taken into the heavens.

If you are a stickler for Biblical confirmation, remember that Elijah was taken up into heaven in a "chariot of fire...by a whirlwind." Later the same prophet was seen along with Moses at the Transfiguration as Jesus stood ready to travel skyward, His robe shining so brilliantly that it resembled the sun. If Elijah could ascend to heaven without dying, it's entirely possible that many of us—or our whole planet—will find ourselves transported there in this New Age so many have prophesied will come.

The Great Battle and a Rejoicing

According to religious scholars, before this millennium of peace there, however, will be a great battle in which the forces of good—the Christ forces—will combat the forces of evil led by the mighty Satan. A fierce, fever pitched battle will be waged in which all sorts of science fiction-like weapons will be used to engulf the planet, and everyone still alive on it, in a literal ball of fire. Millions—no, billions—will be incinerated as God judges our worth, and prepares to cleanse the planet so that a "new heaven and a new earth" can be built from the ashes. Those that have been taken from the Planet will be returned to find a glorious kingdom as described by John in the "New International Version" of the Bible:

"I saw a new heaven and a new earth, for the first heaven and the first earth has passed away, and there was no longer any sea. I saw the Holy City, the new Jerusalem, coming down out of heaven from God, prepared as a bride beautifully dressed for her husband. And I heard a loud voice from the throne saying, 'Now the dwelling of God is with men, and He will live with them. They will be His people, and God Himself will be with them and be their God. He will wipe every tear from their eyes. There will be no more death or mourning or crying or pain, for the old order of things has passed away.'"

Now if God is not talking about a merging of dimensions, a blending of our physical realm with heaven, then what is He speaking of? It seems to me that the meaning of Revelations is as clear as the nose on your face and can hardly be interpreted in any other fashion.

The reason why those who have passed on have been seen onboard UFOs now becomes more evident. The operators of these shining neon lights are not of the physical, but exist in higher—more heavenly—realms and dimensions. Because of their advanced spiritual state they no longer have to dwell in physical bodies, but can take on any appearance that they so choose. Many of the aliens that have been encountered may look remarkably humanoid in appearance, but that is because they can disguise themselves so as not to frighten those they contact. Their true essence is pure light and they, like the angers of the scriptures, can travel the universe and be anywhere instantaneously, whether it be on earth in a farmer's field, or in God's heavenly realms. After we have died they can "pick up" certain souls whose mission has been accomplished on earth in the physical sense and who are ready to go on to more celestial things.

Gloria Lee and the Space Brothers

The late Gloria Lee was a very attractive woman in her mid- thirties who rode the skies as a stewardess for one of the major airlines. In her off duty hours, Gloria had another, more loftier side to her personality. Claiming to have met spiritually advanced beings from other worlds, Gloria would meditate for hours on end, during which time these entities of cosmic good will would channel messages through her.

Much of what they had to say has been retained in a small spiral bound volume titled Why *We Are Here* (available from Inner Light Publications for $10.95). Several of the discourses confirm this impending merger of earth with the heavens, as well as explaining further the nature of spiritual beings said to exist throughout this solar system and others.

"The world we live in is physical in a sense," Gloria's alien friend stated" "Perhaps not to you for your eyes cannot see us. The world we live in is etheric and is in the higher ethers of the physical plane. Your science knows only the three lower ethers. We exist in the four higher ethers, but also reside in the three lower as our plane of life encompasses the whole."

As for the coming New Age, the interdimensional being went on thusly: "In your Golden Age love will reign supreme, the same brotherly love your teachers wanted so much to teach you through the ages. Now, this will become a reality. You will easily feel what you should towards each other in this Christ vibration.

"Gradually this will become stronger and stronger. In time, your planet will raise itself out of this lower physical and become one with us. Then all the solar system will rejoice as brothers in love with God...To you our worlds would be the most wonderful you could see. The worlds we see in all the universe have not been as inharmonious as yours. The planets in our solar system will once again be in harmony when your planet moves into a higher vibration. Then you will really begin to see what a difference this will make to your civilization."

Other space contacts have espoused pretty much the same sort of cosmic philosophy,regardless if the person being contacted lives in America, China, Brazil or Africa. Indeed, there seems to be an overall universality in the majority of these communications from more advanced beings.

The Case of Pauline Sharp

"I asked when the great holocaust was to come. The spirit force showed me.

"As the years rolled past, the light above became brighter and stronger...I saw a black cloud cover the earth so thickly that nothing could be seen. This would be the fulfillment of the prophecy concerning the three days and three nights of darkness that would envelop the planet, occurring through the grace of our merciful God. It would be when the two realms, the third and the fourth dimensions, already increasingly intermingling, would merge so that man on earth would be able to see many forms of fourth dimensional life. But it would be too much for most people to see this all at once, and so the darkness to permit gradual adaptation.

Then a sun burst will shake the entire western hemisphere.

"Finally when the Aquarian Age has become fully operative, each planet revolving around the sun of our solar system will rotate at a different rate than presently, thus changing the length of days on each planet. The day of earth will be closer to twenty-eight and one-half hours."

This vision is but one of many hundreds regarding future land changes and prophecies which have come through Pauline Sharp, who respectfully requests that she be addressed by her spiritual name, Yolanda. Before her abilities became more pronounced to receive messages from evolved, super, non-physical beings, Yolanda was a successful businesswoman. Today, she heads an international society which promotes world peace and brotherhood. Mark Age Associations (Box 290388, Ft. Lauderdale, FL 33329) publishes news and information in preparation for what they say is the Second Coming and the New Age of Aquarius.

We are now, Yolanda states matter of factly, in the final cleansing period, preparatory to the much discussed Golden Age. This is the long prophesied "Harvest Period," the age when she says all error will be swept from earth and from the minds of those men who would remain as they are now.

"For the earth, and all on it, are even now in the process of being transmuted—raised to a higher vibration. We are now entering the Fourth Dimension, wherein all that exists on earth, and the earth itself, will exist in a higher state of evolution."

There will be, and according to Yolanda are, even now in process, many changes in all forms of life. It is to be considered "a natural step in the evolutionary progress of a planet, and will take place regardless of life existing on it." The many and varied earth changes already in effect, as well as the weather patterns and other related phases, are but small examples of how the entire earth is to be changed for this "Aquarian Age."

"These changes," according to Yolanda, "are increasingly evident in man himself. They have brought many to the realization that there is a need a vast change taking place these days. Body structures are being affected. New and undiagnosable ailments (such as AIDS) and body conditions are perplexing nearly everyone. These are due to the vibrational changes—and to what each one is, or is not, doing about them." Also in this New Age period many are experiencing "strange mental and psychic experiences, keeping them secret in fear that others will classify them as unbalanced, neurotic or hysterical. But those who know the causes and work with the changes are experiencing dramatic favorable results. Those who do not understand them, or will not act accordingly when they do know, are going through many painful trials."

Yolanda points out that the Bible tells us, "The old men will have

109

dreams and the young men will have visions and they will prophesy the ending of an age."

Hundreds of thousands of persons all over the world, Yolanda claims, are having an outpouring of this Spirit, "and it is increasing rapidly and dramatically all the time. This is the age of marks, in which many varied signs of the times alert man to the fact that it is indeed the latter-day or the Mark-Age period.

While many have kept quiet about their unusual experiences and demonstrations of spiritual talents, now many are telling of them.

In the prophecies concerning the coming cataclysms, Yolanda is quick to point out, nowhere is mention made of the end of the world. Instead, she does foresee numerous cataclysms throughout the world "as the planet and all on it are transmuted into the higher frequency vibration of the fourth dimension.. Nor are all these cataclysms to be purely physical but many are to take mental and emotional forms.

The reason for these changes, Yolanda explains is, "to cleanse and to prepare the planet for the new or golden age which already has dawned. There have been and are to be those earth changes necessary to renew the land or to furnish new lands for the coming era. However, many of even these, and certainly all of the mental and emotional cataclysms, would not have been necessary had man here risen into his spiritual consciousness. For then he would have known this is a pre-ordained evolvement for this planet, preparatory to one for the entire solar system, and would have known and would have been told how to make the change properly. Also, he would not have created the tremendous errors which have to be cleansed, both within himself and the nature kingdoms."

Looking around us, we see many signs that man is awakening from a cosmic sleep or dream of thousands of years duration. When Tim and I first got involved in this field, many of the aspects of what can loosely be defined as New Age, and are now pretty much accepted, were put down by those still in a state of slumber. Few people, for example, believed that a person's health could be positively affected by the food that they ate. You were a weirdo or—at best—a fadist if you were into not eating meat. Vitamins were thought to have no beneficial value, and exercise was only for athletes until Jane Fonda and Richard Simmons made aerobics, doing situps, and yoga an enjoyable experience that anyone could participate in by watching early morning television. Today, thanks to Shirley MacLaine's best seller *Out On a Limb* you don't automatically get locked up if you express a belief in reincarnation, UFOs, and healthful living.

It is not just by "coincidence" that such subjects are now being brought into the open. The residents of higher dimensions and of the heavens realm are trying to awaken us spiritually as they know of the changes in vibration and density that will soon be changing our lives. They want us to be ready for these events so that we will not be swept away in the tide of negativity that has encircled our earth like a dense cloud for centuries.

Yes, there will be a blending of dimensions, and it will be a great day like no other in the history of humankind.

Electronic Transmissions from the Spirit Realms

Mark Macy is the head of the INIT-US, which stands for the International Network for Instrumental Transcommunication, a group of researchers co-operating under an ethical umbrella to bring the public up to the minute data provided by residents of the spirit realms via telephone, TV signal, computer, and other electronic means.

In fact, Macy maintains that engineers operating from other realms and dimensions who once resided here on the Earth are now working together from the "other side" to provide us with the necessary evidence —via up-to-the-minute electronic transmissions—that death is not the end of our existence as individual spiritual souls. Apparently, any number of broadcasts have been made to date from this dimension along side our own, and physical apports have even "come through" a kind of screen door that separates our world from the "hereafter."

The following article is reprinted from *Psychic News,* Britain's oldest and most respected spiritual publication, and details the INIT's work with Macy at the helm. Mark says that he is convinced that "many people are looking in the wrong direction for intelligent life beyond Earth; rather than outward into the physical universe, we'd have better luck looking inward into subtler dimensions that exist all around us all the time."

Readers who are interested in furthering their knowledge of this form of communication with heavenly realms may contact the INIT directly at Box 11036, Boulder, CO 80301, and request information on their publications which include the book *Conversations Beyond the Light.*

• • •

My country's two main media exports this year have been the O.J. Simpson trial and the glossy TV series, *Baywatch* (also known as "Babewatch"), leaving the impression that much of the world views life in the

USA as something of a circus. So I wish to thank PN and its editor Tim Haugh for this opportunity to spread the word of instrumental transcommunication (ITC) in a good light.

Hopefully this report on some rather exciting and serious research will help in its own small way to offset the balance of the more sensational media.

I also appreciate Tim's two articles which appeared in February and provided an excellent background to the work being done.

A Brief Overview of Instrumental Transcommunication

Most readers of PN are familiar with research into the electronic voice phenomenon which has been under way since the 1950s in Europe, the USA and elsewhere. Experimenters have been finding very weak voices on their audio tapes lasting one to two seconds.

In the 1980s, things began to happen which indicated that the research was becoming less of a voice phenomenon and more of a means of conveying significant information in the form of text, voices and pictures from the worlds of spirit to Earth.

Klaus Schreiber, a German experimenter with strong psychic skills, received instructions from his invisible friends to turn on the TV to an empty channel and aim a video camera at the set. The result was a picture of his deceased daughter Karin.

Soon he was receiving other paranormal images, including a picture purported to be that of great scientist, Albert Einstein, with whom Schreiber claimed to be in telepathic contact.

After Schrieber's death in 1986, he began assisting his earthside colleagues from the other side of the veil. In the summer of 1990, experimenters received two pictures in their computer, one of Schreiber himself and the other of his new home in the astral worlds. The messages accompanying the pictures said:

"Klaus S. as we all know him but now in a new world...These pictures are from Klaus. One shows the house in which he now lives together with his family members.

"For months of earth time Klaus was on a path of investigating his surroundings. Many new arrivals make up for what they could not complete on Earth. Klaus is again experimenting with picture transmission and sends out pictures at random in the hope that his friends on Earth will receive them."

In 1985, Maggy and Jules Harsch-Fishbach began their experiments in Luxembourg, and they soon built up the interdimensional support with deceased ITC pioneer Konstantin Raudive. He had joined a spirit group calling itself "Timestream," which was being assembled with the intent of ushering in a new generation of contacts between "heaven" and earth.

In the autumn of 1986 a new voice joined the sessions. It was a high-pitched, computer-like voice that was almost too perfect to be human. During one session the group asked a question about God, and the high-pitched voice interrupted:

"Please address this question to me."
And Maggy asked, "Who exactly ARE you?"
Came the reply:
"We are what we are. It is not easy to explain to you. I am not an energy being, not a light being. I was never human, never an animal, and was never incarnate. Neither am I God!

"You are familiar with the popular picture of two children walking across a bridge. Behind them is a being that protects them. This is what I am to you but without wings. If you insist on giving me a name, call me Technician."

As months passed, Technician astounded the researchers with his exceptional knowledge of electronics, physics, mathematics, astronomy, general science, history and the future.

He had a memory like a living computer and spoke many languages. Here is one message that came from Technician:

"Fear of death is one of the most distressing concepts of human culture. It is based on the conscious belief that your bodily existence offers life and security, which it never wants to lose.

"Fear of death therefore is evidence of the mind having lost its roots. It shows a spiritual being who has far removed itself from its higher self.

"You owe this mentality largely to an intellectual and scientific way of thinking. It wants all thoughts reduced to a comprehensible level of material existence.

"Heaven is in man and those who have heaven within themselves go to heaven. Heaven is in all those who recognize what is of God and let themselves be guided by the Divine.

"This priority and basic concern of every religion has always been the acknowledgement of God!"

Since then, Technician has played a key role in the unfoldment of ITC on earth, always careful to stay in the background while directing and protecting the human experimenters on both sides of the veil.

Without the involvement of Technician and other higher beings in the project, ITC would not be advancing as quickly nor as safely as it is today.

This all sounds a bit absurd to many people today, but is it really?

How Does ITC Work?

A decade of careful, well-documented experiments and many helpful hints from our invisible colleagues have given us an emerging picture of a reality that is quite alien to modern, civilized man.

Before understanding the inner workings of ITC, a person must first understand this broadened view of life. Not necessarily accept it (as it may rub against some very sacred, very personal beliefs) but at least understand it.

Over the years, mystics of the East, science fiction writers and parapsychologists of the West have offered glimpses of this strange reality to a public and a scientific establishment that has remained largely skeptical.

They tell us stories of people dematerializing from one spot and rematerializing elsewhere, of people overcoming gravity, causing their bodies to rise. They talk of invisible dimensions, teeming with life, superimposed over our own physical plane. Stories are told of material objects made to move or change with thoughts.

Others speak of mystics emitting a flow of oil or a tailing of ash from the palms of their hands, of large, disc-shaped objects appearing mysteriously in the sky, then blinking out. Cases arise of people projecting their mental images onto photographic film. There are haunted houses, spirit possessions, apports...

And now comes ITC, the use of electronic equipment to get long messages and clear images from the invisible worlds of spirit.

For those businessmen, bankers, laborers and engineers alive on Earth today who wish to keep both feet planted firmly on the ground, it is most effective simply to draw a line between themselves and all of these phenomena. It can be very unsettling to venture across that line into the tangled jungle of other-worldly situations.

Why is it unsettling?

For one thing, as we look beyond that line, we begin to realize that life is rather complex. Our physical universe seems to be superimposed on other universes, like radio and TV signals that are all jumbled together in the same room. And like these signals, each universe or dimension has its own laws due to its frequency or vibratory rate.

So, in the quest for extraterrestrial life, we realize that our astronomers may be looking in the wrong direction; instead of outward to the stars, perhaps they should be looking inward into subtler dimensions that exist right here, all around us.

Other sciences are also looking the wrong way in many cases, and that is not reassuring.

As we cross the line into the paranormal, our sense of linear time—past, present and future—begins to fade away. So when we talk of reincarnation, we are no longer talking of past lives and future lives, but of *concurrent* lives.

In the spirit worlds, or subtler dimensions, we are told that everything unfolds at once into a multidimensional panorama in a way that is impossible for most people on Earth to fathom.

Our sense of distance fades away. Space, like time, is said to be a fleeting aberration of the physical dimension. An illusion.

Someday, we are told, we will indeed have vehicles that "fade away" into a subtler dimension, move as quickly as thought, and "fade back" into the physical realm, perhaps at a destination many light-years away from the point of departure.

As we cross the line into the paranormal, the very ground on which we walk—as solid as it seems—begins to fade away into the illusion (which Hindus have warned us for thousands of years it really is!).

That, dear readers, begins to set up a framework in which we can begin to understand the inner workings of ITC.

It would be nice if we could just turn on a TV, computer or radio, or pick up the telephone, and get messages and images from the spirit worlds, but unfortunately it's not that simple. In fact, ITC success depends on some rather complex variables.

In July I visited my friends the Harsch-Fishbachs in Luxembourg. We sat around a configuration of radios and received a long message from Konstantin Raudive. As the hissing white noise of the radios faded out, Dr. Raudive's voice faded in. His first statement was this:

"It can only work when the vibrations of those present are in complete harmony and when their aims and intentions are pure."

And another comment made more recently, again, in Luxembourg:

"Dear friends, as you have already been told by the Technician, should we not be able to anchor transcommunication in this century it will most certainly happen in the next one. An apparatus will be functioning when unity of mind is achieved among researchers. Each of us is responsible for ourselves. This is Konstantin Raudive."

So, that seems to be one of the ITC puzzle pieces. There must be harmony, pure intentions, and unity of mind among experimenters before ITC can work.

The following statement by Swejen Salter might provide the second piece of the puzzle:

"We regret that there are not more stable ITC bridges, but the contact field of the experimenter contributes most to this. It is the very reason why we cannot reach some individuals through radio, TV or computer. Your linear thinking makes contacts more difficult to us and with us."

Our spirit colleagues encourage us to move our minds into a more timeless reality, a quality that seems to be closely associated with what we typically call "psychic skills."

So, from these messages I would conclude the following:

▲ ITC works best when it involves a group of psychically sensitive people whose vibrations are in complete harmony and whose aims and intentions are pure.

▲ It does not work so well when it involves one good psychic with his or her equipment.

▲ ITC does not work with a group of great psychics who are jealous or resentful of each other, because jealousy, resentment and other such feelings create status that disrupts all communications across dimensions. So does hostile skepticism.

I am beginning to realize that ITC does not involve an individual here on Earth communicating with a person in the spirit world, although that's the way it may seem to us today.

I think it is really a group of people on Earth working with a team of spirit beings—and they are all in one mind. They all feel and live that openness.

The ITC experimenters, their supporters, their spirit colleagues, and all the equipment on both sides of the veil, are all part of a single system. They are one. When that situation becomes widespread, I believe we will start seeing good ITC contacts around the world on a regular basis.

We do know that the hardware or equipment involved in ITC is a very minor consideration on ITC work today. The experimenters who concentrate purely on the technical of ITC are getting the poorest results.

Those who take the time to nurture ties with their friends, loved ones and colleagues in the spirit world are those who are attracting capable help from the Other Side.

And make no mistake. At the present time all the technology for advanced ITC contacts is being assembled on the other side of the veil, not here on Earth.

That will certainly change in the future, but for the time being we lack the technologies that deal with life energies. I'm talking about equipment that reacts to our thoughts and attitudes.

Meanwhile, the best we on Earth can do to facilitate the spread of ITC is to be aware of and nurture the contact field. This is a field of life energy (chi, shakti, psi, subtle energy, cosmic energy, Holy Spirit, etc.) that is automatically formed whenever two or more beings develop an awareness of each other. It is formed on our attitudes, thoughts, beliefs and feelings.

In ITC, a strong contact field is built over time between a team of experimenters on Earth and a team of spirit colleagues. It is this inter-dimensional energy field that acts as a sort of etheric power supply to make ITC contacts possible.

But enough of this technical information. I'll continue this article with some of the recent contacts my colleagues in Luxembourg have received.

The Latest ITC Evidence

As more people inform themselves about ITC and new contacts are experienced worldwide, the phenomenon continues to grow. Last year saw a spread of ITC telephone contacts beyond Europe.

On January 14 of last year, I received a phone call from our spirit colleague Konstantin Raudive announcing the creation of a new ITC bridge to the US.

A week later my colleague, ITC pioneer George Meek, received a call at his home. On the same day, researchers Sarah Estep and Walter Uphoff were called by Raudive, and a few weeks later, Hans Heckmann got a call. Within three months, more than a dozen calls were reported by the five of us in the States.

Our colleagues in Brazil and Sweden also began to receive calls from Konstantin Raudive announcing the spread of ITC bridges.

Before long, accusations of a hoax began to surface. After all, such contacts made across public networks could easily be faked.

The accusations came not from the scientific community, as one might guess, but from within the ranks. Several long-time voice experimenters in Germany and the USA, who have never received such long, clear messages just would not believe that they were legitimate …despite independent confirmations of these international, interdimensional calls at other receiving stations.

One such confirmation came on February 20, a month after the first call to the States. German researcher Adolf Homes received a computer message:

"Dear Colleague Adolf Homes. I herewith confirm my own contacts with Mr. Malkhoff (in Germany) and Mr. Meek and Mr. Macy in America.

"More contacts have been made successfully in China and Japan by telephone and fax. Our tests are necessary because humanity is in a state of being—created by itself—which is negative for us to the point that we cannot influence consciousness.

"We therefore ask you to encourage people to open their psychic barriers to a greater extent. Only then is there a chance for us to continue contacts via radio receivers, televisions and computers.

"Unfortunately messages from our side by telephone and fax do not suffice to make clear to humanity our reality as one of many realities. This is Konstantin Raudive."

Homes' computer was and is hooked up to nothing but the power outlet in the wall. No modems or networks. So unless Homes himself were perpetrating an elaborate hoax, his computer message from Raudive is good, solid evidence for the legitimacy of the phone calls.

All colleagues of Adolf Homes know him to be an honest, serious researcher.

Then, as soon as the phone calls began to stir up excitement, they ended just as abruptly. Our colleague in Brazil, Sonia Rinaldi, received a phone call from Konstantin Raudive late last month,but otherwise the lines everywhere have been still.

Except, of course, in the main experimental stations in Luxembourg and Germany which continue to get contacts of various kinds on a regular basis.

The Luxembourg experimenters have been told several times during recent contacts that ITC is presently entering a new phase.

During this phase, the people interested in ITC will be given time to digest the information already received. How they come to feel about ITC will determine how Spirit will proceed in the future.

On December 17 last year, Konstantin Raudive confirmed this through an equipment configuration in Luxembourg called Burton-Bridge II:

"The continuation of the project will be decided by higher beings.

"They currently observe the attitudes and reactions of people concerning ITC.

"You can look at it as sort of a higher discussion. These discussions have been going on since 1994 your time. These higher beings do not know earth time. A few minutes of discussion on our side may be comparable to months or even years on earth. If these beings give me permission I will announce myself again by the same means."

The impression I'm getting from all this is that there is some serious concern among higher beings over the state and fate of the planet. I believe they see great power in ITC as a means of shaping our destiny, and they are trying to see that the power is not misused in its early stages.

Incidentally, before I became involved in ITC I didn't even believe in the existence of higher beings. Now I have no doubts whatsoever, but that is a story in itself, and I do not wish to digress from the focus of this article. If all this is still a stretch for you, please bear with me.

Apports

Since 1992 Maggy and Jules Harsh-Fishbach of Luxembourg have received apports—the materialization of physical objects—from time to time in addition to the text, voices and pictures they receive on a more regular basis.

I will discuss them only briefly, as physical objects mean less to me than insights. Our physical world has countless objects scattered about, but fewer good ideas that can raise the love-and-wisdom quotient (just my opinion, of course).

First apport. My Luxembourg friends like to relax by travelling to old fortresses and castles and studying history.

In the Spring of 1993, they visited a museum in Virton, Belgium, which unfortunately was closed and when returning to the empty parking lot found an old Luxembourg coin next to the car. They were reasonably certain that it had not been there when they had arrived.

Second apport. In April last year, while visiting the fortress Bollendorf in Germany, suddenly in the air, about five yards above them, a small, bright object seemed to form. It rotated with great speed and spun around its own axis.

The object, because of its rapid spin, seemed to stay in the air for a few moments and then fell at their feet with a clinking sound. The coin was warm to the touch, and there was no one around.

One side of the coin carried the inscription, "LUDOV. XVI. D. GRATIA." On the other side was a coat of arms with three lillies and the inscription, "1791 FRANCAIE ET NAVARRAE REX."

The next day, Jules and Maggy found the following paranormal text in their computer:

"Congratulations! You have found one end of the tunnel. At the other end is what you are looking for in the form of metal. You may look at the goal you reached yesterday as the final results of your trips and excursions.

"The second end will be the product of further development. Healings and your continuing path of life are connected with it, as everything is connected with each other and becomes one.

"Be guided by your inner self and you will reach the goal. I preferred this apport to a voice contact and we advanced by it. I shall still call you next week at a good time for both of us. Will give the exact time on Monday. All my love and Tschuk, Swejen."

A few days later Swejen told Maggy that the apport was a text from their side to practice the passage of objects through the "tunnel."

Swejen: "The coin is from the year 1791 during the reign of Louis XVI."

Maggy: "Have people helped with the experiment who lived during that time?"

Swejen: "Of course, they are the part of Group Timestream. Many became interested in ITC after you visited Varennes in autumn 1993."

Maggy: "Did the apports have to happen exactly at this place and at this point in time or could we have been somewhere else?"

Swejen: "It had to be this place at exactly this time. It is a place you have to drive to again before you will experience any more materializations."

Maggy: "Did we have to search further to the north or the south?"

"Swejen: "I cannot tell you yet, but it was important at this time for you to be here. It was a test to activate the tunnel on both sides."

Maggy: "If I understand correctly, a similar method can also be used for the healing?"

Swejen: "Yes, exactly."

Maggy: "But apparently you cannot tell me anything more about that now."

Swejen: "Not now, we have to wait. But I can tell you that the moment when you were at one end of the tunnel where the apport could take place, we were able to make measurements and practically were able to make you visible as a hologram on our side."

Maggy: "Oh, really?"

Swejen: We shall try something similar in the final phase of the healing process. We shall tell you more about it soon."

Third apport. A few days later, on April 29, the Harsch-Fishbachs drove to Larochette and visited the castle there.

Nothing happened, so they walked to the terrace of a nearby hotel. When Maggy momentarily lifted her handbag off the table there was an object on the table that was not there moments earlier.

It was a thin, silver-colored coin with the inscription, "1702 LVD XIII D G FRETNAVARRAE."

Fourth apport. On May 11 the couple were sitting outside Falkenstein castle. Two old trees stood on either side of the bench. Suddenly there was a loud rustling in the branches, and an object dropped out of the leaves. Carefully, Jules spread apart the grass and found a golden bracelet.

Arriving home at 11:15 PM they found a message from experimenter Adolf Homes from Rivenich, Germany, on their telephone answering device. His deceased mother Elise Karoline had notified him that Maggy and Jules had found her bracelet which she lost under "mysterious circumstances" in the year 1933 near castle Falkenstein.

Nobody besides spirit colleague Swejen Salter had known about their trip to Falkenstein, so it was evidential indeed to receive this message from Adolf Homes upon arriving home.

Homes is receiving regular contacts from his departed mother Elise Karoline by the same means by which Swejen Salter contacts the Luxembourg couple. Elise Karoline and Swejen have been cooperating regularly in the spirit world.

Maggy called Adolf Homes to confirm that they had found his mother's bracelet.

The following morning Maggy found a message from Elise Karoline Homes in her computer. It ran:

"The bracelet is for you, Maggy. It is a gift from me. I shall notify my son. He is happy about it. Elise Karoline Homes."

Fifth apport. On May 15 the couple turned on the computer, and a small object dropped down from the ceiling, hit the keyboard and fell on the floor. They found a pendant in the shape of a face mask of white and gold color.

Four days later they discovered a message on their computer which included a note from Swejen Salter:

"The 'Peduccio' is from the Lombardian group."

Swejen explained that the name "Peduccio" referred to the apported gold pendant.

Sixth apport. On July 2 they visited the ruins of the fortress in Kronenburg, Germany, which once housed a "Commandment" of the Knights Templars.

Near the entrance of the town they experienced the materialization of a gold pendant in the shape of a cross. On our side a small ornament is engraved with a design, on the other side the name "JERUSALEM" appears.

A few days later Konstantin Raudive came through on Burton-Bridge II:

"The pendant came to you from the former French Knight Templar Airenet who has joined Group Timestream."

Apparently Airenet had participated in the crusade to Jerusalem.

Seventh apport. On the evening of October 31 last year, Maggy and Jules set out for a place of pilgrimage in the south of Luxembourg. They arrived at 8:50 PM at a grotto which was cut out of rock.

While they were still trying to interpret the inscription in the dark, a small metallic object "formed" itself above their heads and seemed to mix with the rain drops. The glittering object twirled across Maggy's right shoulder and came to rest before their feet.

They picked it up and recognized a finely crafted golden pendant depicting the head of an eagle.

Eighth apport. Another gold pendant, bigger than the others, this time depicting a flying eagle, arriving in the Harsch-Fishbach apartment on the morning of December 17, 1994, while Maggy was busy with the care of their two parrots.

The object seemed to fall off the ceiling. The parrots were excited and nervously flapped their wings.

Maggy discovered text in the computer which announced a spirit group calling itself Group Eagle. Swejen Salter later explained:

"This is a new group. They deal mostly with the compression of objects of materialization. Lorenzo Tellarini, Umberto Ursi, and Cornelia Bandi are in charge. They hope you like the object."

Contacts

On November 10, last year, Maggy found a picture and letter in her computer. It ran as follows:

"The entity who was called Anne Guigne during her lifetime and left Earth on January 14, 1922, showed herself on October 10 at 10:12 AM via TV in Rivenich and through your scanner program in Luxembourg. Her message is as follows:

"As a little girl in France I got very ill. I was an important source of information. Through spiritual insight and prayer I learned from the omnipotence that I was better able to understand the things I needed to know here in the third level and could do more for mankind from here than on Earth.

"I desired the change into a multidimensional world and was allowed a fast passing over to a world some memory of which was still alive in me. It is the same beautiful world you have heard about from others like me.

"There are 35,000 to 40,000 children dying daily on earth. My task became clear to me. Together with other scientists, physicians and theologians, I am in charge of a group for the protection of all the newborn life. We are particularly concerned about those who have to die as children."

"As you know, the conception of guilt does not exist here. However, we do not understand your overall attitude towards these entities who voluntarily walk the path of incarnation and are part of all that is.

"In particular it is your consciousness that bears the responsibility for your children,not only by evolutionary law but also by the natural laws of all that is.

"Be aware therefore that the wars and violent events caused by you, and from which particularly your innocent children suffer, are not sparing you part of the so-called purgatory. Just the opposite.

"Every debt you shoulder by sacrificing your own flesh and blood to wars is adding to the misery, and suffering that awaits you.

"The more you create your own hell on Earth by your criminal deeds and negligence, the less it will be diminished for you here later. Therefore consider carefully what you do.

"We know that those among you who are actively pursuing ITC in a positive manner are not evil people. We want to encourage you to oppose crimes against the defenseless. You can do this by leading an honest life in accordance with spiritual cooperation.

"Anne Guigne is greeting you, especially the children."

The following short message accompanied the picture:

"Anne Guigne. Born at Annecy on April 25, 1911. Transition made on January 14, 1922. Guardian angel of Remy."

In conclusion, it needs to be repeated that ITC today is at a crossroads. About the time this goes to press, more than a dozen top ITC researchers from throughout Europe and America will be converging on a meeting hall in the English countryside of Devon to help determine the future path of ITC.

We are told by our spirit colleagues that the outcome of this meeting will have much to do with the spread of ITC in the coming years.

For those of us who see ITC entwined with human destiny, it is not too great an exaggeration to say that we will be helping, in our own small way, to determine the fate of the planet.

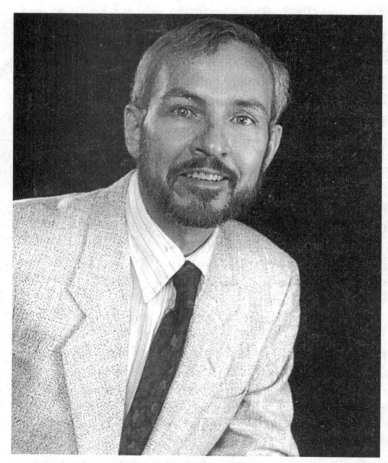

Mark Macy, head of INIT-US (International Network for Instrumental Transcommunication.

Write to Diane, Receive HELP...

For fifteen years, Diane Tessman has led the New Age, guiding ousands of people toward their own personal step in spiritual olution. Through this new understanding and <u>knowing</u>, they have so found new happiness, health, prosperity, and psychic power. ane will be happy to work with <u>you</u>!

Personal Counseling by Diane/Private Channeling by Tibus

Receive astounding guidance and psychic information from Diane ssman and her star guardian, Tibus! This is a written channeling u will cherish all your life - which will also give you valuable guidance in the frightening days ahead. These readings ve worked miracles for thousands of people!

Feel free to write explaining your specifics when you order. ecify if you wish to place emphasis on counseling by Diane or on lepathic communication with Tibus, through Diane. If you do not ecify, Diane and Tibus will share in-put into your personal, ivate counseling which will be a minimum of five single-spaced pe-written pages - just for you!

Diane and Tibus will work with your past and future lifetimes, nancial, love, sex, health, relationship problems, impart your ueprint for the upcoming Earth changes, help in contacting your rsonal guardian, practical counseling for difficulties countered in the world (improving "luck"), and more! $100.00
* We can accept a very limited number of students. After your rst channeling, we will consider this if you wish.

THE CHANGE TIMES QUARTERLY, by Diane Tessman, is published 4

mes a year with urgent transmissions from Tibus, Veritan, ethysta, other members of the Space/Time Intelligence. Current obal crisis are explained, crucial information is given! **Find out e truth with facts which are censored from the regular news dia. CTQ can literally help you survive the times ahead!**

Get the real story on cancer, AIDS, government/negative alien nspiracy, the break up of Antarctica, predictions of floods, akes, info available no where else on UFOs & upcoming meetings tween millions of aliens & humans, & much more! Subscription is 5.00 p/year (4 issues). Current sample copy, $5.00. Write today!

The Star Network Heartline, written monthly by Diane & Tibus

r 15 years, treasured by thousands of Light Workers. Don't miss t, you are not alone! $25 per year. <u>Write for sample copy FREE</u>!
Send $1.00 for **EARTH CHANGES CATALOG** with wonderful, uplifting deos by Diane, incredible channeled manuscripts, and much more!

DIANE TESSMAN, P.O. BOX 352, ST. ANSGAR, IOWA 50472

The following volumes contain previously unknown facts.

HIDDEN TRUTHS THAT CAN NOW BE REVEALE

READ INNER LIGHT'S CONTROVERSIAL SERIES

RELIGIOUS SECRETS EXPOSED

1R. PSYCHIC & UFO REVELATIONS IN THE LAST DAYS by Tim Beckley
What the church does not want you to know concerning: the appearance of the anti-christ; the mass landing of space ships to take the "chosen" to a safe place in space; a forthcoming Polar Shift; graves to be opened and corpses to be gone!; 3 Days of Darkness; Find out which States will be geographically altered and the "safe" places to go to be out of immediate danger. An exact time table indicating when these events will begin to take place and the order in which they will occur. Exact "signs and wonders" to watch for which will indicate that only months are left. - $15.00.

2R. ANGELS OF THE LORD by Art Crockett
Now you can call upon your Guardian Angel for guidance and protection. Answers the questions: Do Angels Walk Amongst Us? Is the War With Satan Still Going On? How Do Angels Travel? What Has Been The Roll of Angels in the History of America? How Do YOU Call Upon Angels For Help? Do UFOs Tie in With the Messengers of God (Billy Graham says they do!) - $15.00.

3R. ARK OF THE COVENANT - GODS SECRET WEAPON by David Medina
If you thought the movie *Raiders of the Lost Ark* was fiction, you're completely wrong. The Ark really existed and had the power of an atomic bomb. Though it was originally constructed to carry the 10 Commandments, you will find out its various other uses. Find out about the "breast plate" the Priests wore consisting of many mystical gems, and how they actually spoke with God and received a direct response. One of the major archaeological finds of all time is about to be made in the Middle East with the recovery of the Ark. Can it be used to battle evil on Earth? - $15.00

4R. SECRET PROPHECY OF FATIMA REVEALED by Tim Beckley & Art Crockett
Who is the "Lady in White" who has appeared over 200 times this century to issue a warning to humankind? What are the mysterious contents of the "Third Prophecy of Fatima" and why has it "officially" never been released? Here are the Miracles & Prophecies of the Blessed Virgin Mary and their importance in the New Age. - $15.00.

5R. PASSPORT TO HEAVEN by Diane Tessman & Timothy Green Beckley
How can you be certain of going to heaven when you die? Is it possible to communicate with the "Next World" now? Can the dead pick up the phone and call the living? How close is Heaven to Earth? Can we go there in a space ship or in a UFO? What is it like living in Heaven - do we eat, have mates, talk with God, sing with angels? - $15.00

6R. WEEPING ANGEL PREDICTION bu Michael X
What is the secret behind the painting of an angel that cries real tears? Is the prophecy surrounding it about to come true? Has it really healed many of those who own a copy of this mysterious piece of art? Comes complete with an 8 x 10 reproduction of the Weeping Angel suitable for framing. See if what others say about this lithograph is true! - $8.00

7R. THE NEW AGE BIBLE - THE HIDDEN TRUTH REVEALED by Dr. John Rodgers
What is the New Age and have we entered it? Are all religions compatible? Is our civilization on a path of higher consciousness or mass destruction? The author says, the New Age "movement" will actually change the course of history and that UFOs are the "Signs of the Heavens", and the Crop Circles the "Mysteries of the Earth". $15.00

8R. REVELATION - THE DIVINE FIRE by Brad Steiger
Is Earth entering a new "vibration?" - What great changes will take place in the immediate future as predicted by Cayce and Nostradamus? What is causing the outbreak of "Holy Spirit", and making people have visions of Mary/Jesus or to channel "higher intelligence"? - $15.00.

❖ ❖ ❖ ❖ ❖ ❖ ❖ ❖ ❖ ❖ ❖ ❖